Teaching Reading Vocabulary

Tom Nicholson

and

Sue Dymock

NZCER PRESS

WELLINGTON 2010

NZCER PRESS
The New Zealand Council for Educational Research
PO Box 3237
Wellington
New Zealand

© Tom Nicholson, Sue Dymock, 2010

ISBN 978-1-877398-62-9

All rights reserved

Design by Lynn Peck, Central Media, Wellington
Printed by Thames Publications, Wellington

Distributed by NZCER Distribution Services
PO Box 3237
Wellington
New Zealand
www.nzcer.org.nz

Contents

Introduction 1

PART 1: THEORY

Chapter 1: A Short History of English Words 8

Chapter 2: Words: The Core Ingredient in Language..............................17

Chapter 3: Catering for Diverse Learners 30

PART 2: PRACTICE

Introduction..44

Chapter 4: Increasing Vocabulary Through Reading...............................46

Chapter 5: Structural Analysis 63

Chapter 6: Constructing Word Meanings With Concept Maps................81

Chapter 7: Exploring the Multiple Meanings of Words 96

Chapter 8: The Dictionary and Thesaurus 117

Chapter 9: Reflections 134

References...137

Introduction

This book is written for teachers but it is useful for anyone who wants to improve their vocabulary. Good readers and writers have a large and diverse vocabulary that gives them a head start on other readers. In reading, it helps not just with comprehension but with learning and remembering new words as well. In writing, it gives precision and depth to the ideas you want to convey.

The Internet is full of ideas and opinions about how best to learn and teach vocabulary, but the research is not so full of certainties. This is partly why we wrote the book, to make sure that the reader is aware of the best, research-based ideas for learning new words, and remembering them, and to explain how to bring those ideas into the classroom.

The New Zealand Curriculum

The importance of vocabulary is emphasised in *The New Zealand Curriculum* (Ministry of Education, 2007). The term *vocabulary* is explicitly mentioned as a teaching objective from Level 3 to Level 8 of the *Curriculum*, and is implicit in Levels 1 and 2. The document repeatedly states that a student needs to be able to use *a range of vocabulary to communicate precise meaning*. The use of the word *precise* is because it is the ability to use the right word to express the right idea or emotion that distinguishes the good writer, and it is the ability to bring to the printed page a depth of vocabulary that enables the good reader to reconstruct the exact and sometimes subtle meanings the author wants to convey.

Vocabulary and the reading and writing standards: What children need to know

Vocabulary is becoming much more visible in the teaching of reading. The Ministry of Education (2009) reading and writing standards (for Years 1–8) set out expectations for reading and writing in terms of what students should be able to handle at each year level. These expectations include vocabulary. Let's look in a bit more detail at these expectations.

As early as Year 2 the standards expect pupils to be able to use vocabulary strategies to learn the meanings of new words; for example, when reading, to use sentence context clues and illustrations to work out the meaning of the word *maize* and understand that it is different to *maze*. In writing about a text topic, such as an article about worm farms, the standards expect that pupils can use vocabulary that is "precise" and "descriptive" (with words such as *sprinkle* and *dampen*).

INTRODUCTION

In Year 4 the reading standards expect students to understand figurative language—such as metaphors, similes and personification—when they come across these vocabulary expressions in text. In writing, the standards expect pupils to draw on a deep vocabulary to use precise words such as *approach*, *stare* and *glance* in their descriptions; in other words, to use vocabulary that can "clearly convey ideas, experiences, or information".

In Year 5 the standards expect students to use contextual and other strategies to unlock the meanings of unfamiliar words, such as *plight* and *black market* in the article "Plight of the Sea Turtle". Pupils are also expected to understand and use topic-specific vocabulary; for example, when writing a report on building a "bottle submarine", they should be able to handle topic-specific words such as *approximately*, *build*, *design*, *prototype* and *suspend*.

In Year 6 the reading standards expect pupils to cope with a significant amount of vocabulary that is unfamiliar to students" when they are reading text. The words and phrases in students' writing are expected to show awareness of topic, register and purpose; that is, they should be able to draw on a rich database of vocabulary inside their heads. Such writing also requires an understanding of how to choose the right word for the right purpose, and how to source these words with a dictionary or thesaurus.

In Years 7 and 8 the standards continue to stress a high-level awareness of vocabulary, with an expectation that students will understand figurative vocabulary such as metaphor, analogy and connotation in their reading and be able to use figurative vocabulary in writing tasks. In Years 7 and 8 the standards emphasise the ability to understand academic and topic-specific vocabulary when reading, and when writing the students are expected to use precise, topic-specific vocabulary and be able to provide the reader of their work with explanations within the text of what these words mean.

Overall, the new reading and writing standards expect pupils to enrich their vocabulary knowledge through reading and be able to draw on this store of words for their writing. Ideas on teaching vocabulary are therefore very relevant to today's classroom—and tomorrow's as well.

Literacy Learning Progressions

The expectations of the Ministry's reading and writing standards are mirrored in the *Literacy Learning Progressions: Meeting the Reading and Writing Demands of the Curriculum* (Ministry of Education, 2010). This document outlines the knowledge and skills Years 1–8 children need in order to make year-appropriate progress and meet the "demands of *The New Zealand Curriculum*" (p. 3). According to the *Progressions*, by the end of the first year of school children should be able to apply "their knowledge of vocabulary in order to understand words as they decode them" (p. 12); by the end of their third year of school they should "know the meaning of some common prefixes and suffixes and understand how they affect the meanings of words" (p. 14). and be "aware of synonyms for and multiple meaning of many common words" (ibid.); by the end of Year 6 they should be able to draw on "knowledge and skills that include: finding and learning the meanings of unknown vocabulary" (p. 16) using a range of strategies and "understanding that words and phrases can have figurative as well as literal meanings" (ibid.); and by the end of Year 8 they should be "using their growing academic and content-specific vocabulary to understand text" (p. 17) and be able to interpret "metaphor, analogy and connotative language" (ibid.). This is knowledge that teachers can teach using the ideas in this book.

The structure of the book

While we are strongly of the opinion that coaching students, giving them productive strategies for building vocabulary, should be based on the best research, our main goal has been to translate this research into practical strategies that classroom teachers can use straight away. We have done this by dividing the book into two sections. In Part 1, that is, Chapters 1 to 3, our goal is to give teachers a theoretical understanding of the nature of the English language, as well as an explanation of the latest research on learning and teaching vocabulary. In Part 2, Chapters 4 to 9, we focus on ideas for translating research into practice.

Vocabulary learning is more than knowing facts

Knowing a word is more than being able to recite a list of facts. There is something hollow, not quite right, about hearing someone explain a word as a list of facts. An example is in the book *Hard Times*, first published in 1862 by Charles Dickens, where the opening pages introduce the teacher, Mr Gradgrind, who believes that education is all about knowing facts: "Now what I want is Facts. Teach these boys and girls nothing but Facts. Facts alone are wanted in life." When he asks for a definition of a *horse*, one of the children, Sissy, whose father worked with horses in a circus, could have described a horse in a way that brought all her experiences to the definition, but this was not what Mr Gradgrind wanted. What he wanted were the scientific facts, which one of his pupils, Bitzer, gave him: "Quadruped. Graminovorous. Forty teeth, namely twenty four grinders, four eye-teeth, and twelve incisive. Sheds coat in the spring; in marshy countries, sheds hoofs too. Hoofs hard but requiring to be shod with iron. Age known by marks in mouth." The definition is all about teeth and hoofs. It is as if a horse is an alien creature, not the animal that we usually think of as a *horse*.

INTRODUCTION

This is *not* the way we think vocabulary should be taught or learnt. When we first acquire meaning for the word *horse*, it might be associated with seeing a picture of a horse, or watching a horse on television, the experience of having seen or touched or ridden a horse, or even having it mentioned in a conversation or in a text. What we store in memory are key features that enable us to relate a *horse* to other animals we know about, but also note features that make it different. We store an image of a horse in memory, how to pronounce the word horse and (if we can read) we store the written form of the word. We argue in this book that words are best learnt if our understanding can include all these things.

How to stick words in memory

In this book we describe how best to come across new words, which we think is best done through reading, but also how to glue those words in memory so that we do not lose them. We argue that we learn much new vocabulary, and enrich existing vocabulary, simply by reading or listening, but that if we want to glue those words in memory it is useful to think about words as we read them, to ask questions like: What language is it from? What meaningful parts is it made of? How does it connect to other words we already know? What is its emotive side? and Is it meant to be understood literally or metaphorically? This does not necessarily mean reaching for the dictionary, though you can do this, and in the book we do champion making more use of the much-maligned dictionary. Learning a new word in a conscious way is really a mind set, where you can stand back from a word, and think about it in several ways at once, in ways that help to keep that word in memory.

The research is compelling that we best remember new words by reading them, and then associating them with some kind of image if at all possible, linking them to other known words, linking their written form to their pronunciation, and to their spelling. We may not have to do all these things but they all help, especially for the struggling reader; for example, writing down just a few new words (not too many) each day on a piece of paper when they occur in reading, looking up their meanings, pronouncing them and using them in speech, all act like glue on a poster on a wall—to help new words to stick in memory.

Not everyone has a wide vocabulary

Vocabulary is critical to success in school and in life. It is easy to overlook how important vocabulary is in school. Books and other reading material that children encounter in school can contain more than 100,000 different words yet the average five-year-old only knows 10,000 different words, and some, especially those from homes with few books, or from poverty or second-language backgrounds, know far fewer than that. By the end of primary school most children know 25,000 words and by the end of high school 40,000 words. This is good, but there are still many words to learn. Knowing the meanings of many thousands of words is essential for oral and written literacy. The child who can understand and use effectively many different words has a much better chance of becoming a successful reader, writer and communicator.

What this book covers

The book discusses current research on vocabulary and presents research-based strategies teachers can use for increasing students' word level knowledge. It begins with a short history of the English language that explains the richness and complexity of English: that it is a polyglot, that it has borrowed words from at least 100 languages and that knowing where a word comes from helps to remember it. It also explains what it means to know a word, how words are learnt and how this is relevant to diverse learners.

The practical focus of the book is on suggesting ideas for teaching and learning new vocabulary, ranging from ideas for extensive reading, shared and guided reading with discussion, webbing and weaving, semantic classification (e.g., synonyms, antonyms, denotation, connotation, homographs and homophones, similes and metaphors, idioms and proverbs), using prefixes and suffixes, etymology and the effective use of a dictionary and thesaurus.

Part 1—Theory

In Chapter 1 we give a short history of the English language so as to explain to the reader that English is not just one language. English has been influenced by many languages but when it comes down to it we argue that the student is better off to think of the language as having three main layers of words: Anglo-Saxon, Romance (Latin and French) and Greek. We show how students can compare and contrast these different words with each other.

In Chapter 2, we explore what it means to know a word. The chapter reviews the role vocabulary plays in reading comprehension and also writing, listening and speaking.

In Chapter 3, we describe how to meet the learning needs of all children. Classroom teachers must consider how to cater for children who are gifted, have special needs, who come from homes without books and/or who are learning English as an additional language. This chapter takes a look at what research has to say about teaching vocabulary to diverse learners. We show how to meet the challenge, and recommend the best conditions for learning English vocabulary, including ideas on how to foster the relationship between vocabulary learning in two languages.

Part 2—Practice

In Chapter 4, we explain how a great deal of new vocabulary is learnt through reading. Research suggests that reading, rather than oral language, is the main contributor to vocabulary growth once a child reaches 10 years of age (i.e., Year 5). This chapter explains why reading is an important source of vocabulary. Implications for the classroom teacher are discussed including how to motivate the reluctant reader, as well as the student who can read but does not. We also discuss using contextual clues while reading.

In Chapter 5, we explain how the meanings of many new words can be reconstructed by building them up in terms of their meaningful parts. The chapter discusses how to go about teaching vocabulary through breaking words into parts. Instruction tackles prefixes, suffixes, Latin roots and Greek combining forms.

In Chapter 6, we show how words can be learnt by making links from new words to known words. We describe a small number of useful visual strategies for teaching students how to make links. We cover semantic mapping (i.e., web, weave, thermometer, Venn diagram). Concept maps provide a visual image that aids comprehension.

In Chapter 7, we describe how many words have more than one meaning and how we need to have a set for the multiple meanings of words when we read, otherwise we can get confused. We discuss the multiple meanings of many words, as well as synonyms, antonyms, homographs, homophones, homonyms, idioms and proverbs. Students should be aware that many words have multiple meanings.

In Chapter 8, we discuss the fact that many students do not like using dictionaries and the thesaurus but we argue that we need to find ways to inspire pupils to acquire a love of these amazing resources. We suggest a number of activities to do this.

In Chapter 9, we reflect on what we have tried to achieve in the book. Our aim is to inspire a love of words in our students and we have suggested many activities that we think do this. We hope you enjoy using the book, and that your students do as well, and we would appreciate any feedback you can give us for the future.

PART 1: THEORY

CHAPTER 1

A Short History of English Words

Introduction

In this chapter we discuss a very small and not at all technical part of language: the history of English words, or where English words came from. The vocabulary size of the English language is huge, with more than half a million words. It is important to think about where they came from because if we understand the history of English words we can understand words better.

If we dig into the history of English words what we find is that they come from not just one language but many. One reason for this is that the British Isles were subject to numerous invasions, the invaders each time bringing with them new languages. English has even been called the "language of invasion" (Winchester, 2003).

Another reason for the growth of English is because it was allowed to grow freely. As Calfee and Patrick (1995, p. 70) put it, "Unlike other cultures, we have never said 'no' to a word." That is, English has never experienced censorship as to what words it can include. It is this extensive borrowing that gives English its strength and flexibility. The growth of English has been gradual, extending over more than 1,500 years, but it has grown into a huge number of words.

In terms of teaching vocabulary, it can be useful to think of English in terms of three historical layers. In the top layer, the most recent, we find technical words, borrowed mostly from Greek, which we use in technical areas such as science. In the middle layer are the Romance words, mainly from Latin and French. In the bottom layer are Anglo-Saxon words, spoken by the Germanic tribes who invaded the British Isles in the 5th century and whose language became the basis of English as we know it today (see Figure 1.1).

FIGURE 1.1: THE THREE HISTORICAL LAYERS OF ENGLISH
(Calfee & Associates, 1984)

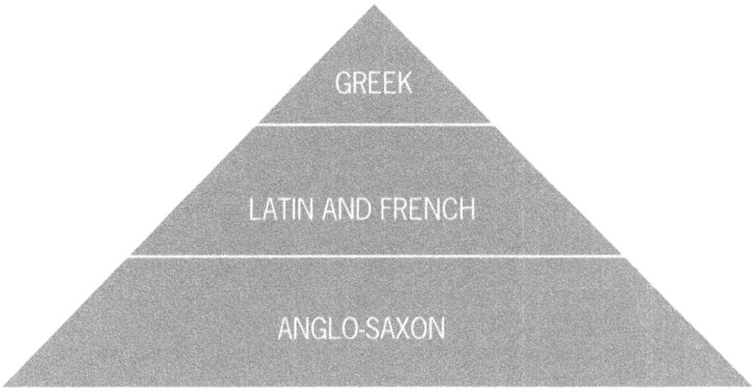

GREEK

LATIN AND FRENCH

ANGLO-SAXON

The scope of the English language

Compared to many languages English is relatively new. When Julius Caesar arrived in Britain in 55 BC English did not exist. The language of the people was Celtic. Five hundred years later "Englisc" (pronounced *English*) was spoken, but it would have been considered a minor language. What's more, Englisc would have been incomprehensible to today's speakers of English. Around the time of the Norman Conquest (1066) English was spoken by approximately 1.5 million people (Barnett, 1962, p. 73). By the 1600s English was the native language of around five to seven million people.

Between 1600 and today English has touched every corner of the globe. English is now spoken as a second language by over 400 million people, and approximately 400 million people speak English as their native language (Baugh & Cable, 2002; Freeborn, 1998; Henry, 2003). English is not the most widely spoken language on earth—Mandarin Chinese takes first place, with at least 900 million speakers—but it is a highly sought-after language. King (2000) estimates that a billion people around the world are learning English as a foreign language.

English has changed considerably over the centuries and it continues to change. All living languages change, and while some changes are quite subtle, others can occur right in front of our eyes. Pronunciations change and new definitions for existing words and phrases are continually being added to our lexicon.

Indeed, the growth in English vocabulary is nothing short of astounding. It is estimated that there were about 50,000–60,000 Anglo-Saxon words, though only a fraction of these survived. By the Middle Ages, English had grown to 100,000–125,000 words. This number doubled during the Renaissance, and it is estimated that the international British, American and Commonwealth English of today comprises approximately 650,000–750,000 words (Nagy & Anderson, 1984; Nist, 1966, p. 8).[1]

Where have these 750,000 words come from? They come primarily from borrowing. English has borrowed (to name just a few) from Hebrew (amen), French (emotion), Inuit (igloo), Italian (volcano, rocket), Arabic (alcohol, magazine), Dutch (golf), Spanish (vanilla, mosquito), American Indian (potato, chocolate) and Hawaiian (ukulele). Few would debate that English is a truly cosmopolitan language (Baugh & Cable, 2002; Nist, 1966; Potter, 1966). Despite this profusion, there are a number of milestones in the history of the development of English that are important to understanding some of the major changes that have occurred, and we will discuss these now.

---

1 See Chapter 6 on the difficulties of counting words.

A chronology of English vocabulary
The emergence of the Anglo-Saxon layer of English

There are six significant events between the 5th and the 20th centuries that had a profound influence on English. Why start at the 5th century? Well, there were other interesting events before that, but in terms of English, we think of its history as only going back 1,500 years, mainly because the language of previous inhabitants had little or no influence on it. English was not the first language used in England. The British Isles have been populated for at least 50,000 years (Claiborne, 1983). The original inhabitants were named Iberians, and did some interesting things; for example, they built Stonehenge. In terms of language, however, the first invaders whose language we know about were the Celts who came to England about 500 years before the birth of Christ (BC), pushed out the Iberians and called themselves Britons (Winchester, 2003).

The arrival of the Angles, Saxons and Jutes

The Celtic language had a minimal effect on English, partly because the Romans, under Claudius, invaded England in AD43 and pushed the Celts back into the west and north of England where their language became the basis of Welsh, Cornish, Scots Gaelic and Irish (Winchester, 2003). There are some Celtic words in English but very few; for example, place names like London and Dover, and rivers like Thames, and that is about it. The Celtic language did merge with the Latin language of the Romans during the 400 or more years of Roman occupation but, when the Romans retreated from England, a new set of invaders in the mid-5th century displaced this hybrid language, partly by killing as many Celts as they could and pushing them back to Wales and Cornwall and the Scottish border (Winchester, 2003).

The new invaders were from parts of Denmark and Germany, and included different tribes—Frisians, Jutes, Saxons and Angles. Over the next 600 years of settlement, which included much war and bloodshed, there emerged a nation called "Englaland" and a language called Anglo-Saxon. This Anglo-Saxon language is what we now call Old English and it generally covers the period from AD450 to 1150.

Readers today would experience great difficulty reading Old English. In fact they would have more success reading French. Words were not only pronounced differently but some characters were different. According to Baugh and Cable (2002), 85 percent of Old English words are no longer in use. However, the 15 percent that did survive form the backbone of Modern English. Anglo-Saxon words are considered the "glue words" in today's English. They hold the language together. Indeed, it is very difficult to write a sentence without an Anglo-Saxon word. According to McCrum, Cran, and MacNeil (1987), the 100 most common words in the English language today are Anglo-Saxon.

Although their vocabulary was simple, the Anglo-Saxons developed a variety of ways of enriching their vocabulary. One way was through self-explaining compounds; that is, by joining two base words. For example, one word, *beadoleoma*, meaning sword, literally translates as "battle light", a concept that was used in Star Wars (Winchester, 2003). Modern English examples of such a compounding strategy include *railway*, *football* and *fibreglass*. Anglo-Saxons also made generous use of prefixes and suffixes. Many of the Anglo-Saxon prefixes are prepositions (e.g., *over-*, *in-*, *under-*). There are about 12 prefixes that were used frequently (e.g., *be-*, *fore-*, *mis-* and *un-*) and a similar number of suffixes (e.g., *-ed*, *-er*, *-ing*, *-ly*, *-s(es)*, *-able*, *-hood*, *-ful*, *-less*, *-ness*, *-ship*, *-ish*) (Henry, 1990).

The emergence of the Latin layer of English

Although we previously noted that the Romans brought Latin words to England, it was a new kind of colonisation, Christianity, that started the increase in Latin words. St Augustine and his 40 Latin-speaking monks brought Christianity, a Latin Bible and a large Latin vocabulary to England in AD 597. The increase in Latin vocabulary occurred gradually between 597 and 1100. Old English was strengthened and enriched, and speakers were able to express more subtle ideas. This phase had an effect on the size of the church vocabulary. While the Anglo-Saxons had *God*, *heaven*, *sin*, *church* and *bishop* in their vocabulary, St Augustine and his monks brought words such as *altar*, *angel*, *anthem*, *antichrist*, *deacon*, *disciple*, *minister*, *noon*, *nun*, *organ*, *palm*, *pope*, *priest*, *prophet*, *shrine*, *temple* and *relic*. The church also influenced learning: *school*, *master* and *verse* were added during this time. Words associated with clothing also came into the language (*sock*, *cap*, *silk*), along with foods (*pear*, *beet*, *caul* or *cabbage*, *oyster*, *lobster*, *mussel*) and the names of trees and plants (*box*, *pine*, *balsam*, *fennel*, *hyssop*, *lily*, *savory*, *plant*). Why did these particular words come into the language? No one knows why, but Winchester (2003) says that *sock*, for example, a Latin word, perhaps came into English because missionaries had to wear foot coverings to protect them from the English winter.

Scandinavian words and the Vikings

About 200 years later, in AD 793, the Scandinavian Vikings (Norwegians, Swedes and Danes) began raiding and pillaging Britain and hundreds of their words came into English during this time. The influence of these invaders can be seen in the similarity of some Scandinavian words and English words, such as *father* and *mother*, *man* and *wife*. *Town*, *house*, *room*, *ground*, *land*, *summer* and *winter* are also common to English and Scandinavian languages. The languages share colours (*grey*, *green* and *white*), verbs (*come*, *hear*, *ride*, *see*, *set*, *sit*, *smile* and *stand*) and adjectives (*full* and *wise*) (Potter, 1966, p. 31). During the two centuries between the arrival of the Vikings in 793 and William the Conquerer in 1066, the speakers of English and the Scandinavian languages became neighbours. In time they intermarried, and the languages intertwined. Yet the overall impact of the missionaries, the Vikings and the Danes, in terms of English vocabulary, was quite small, about 3 percent of the 50,000 Old English words (Winchester, 2003).

The emergence of the French layer of English—1066 and all that—the Norman conquest

In 1066 William, Duke of Normandy, defeated King Harold at the Battle of Hastings and became King William I of England. This conquest had a profound effect on the language, for many reasons. With the Norman Conquest the official language of England became French. Baugh and Cable (2002) conclude that the Norman Conquest, over the next 300 years, "changed the whole course of the English language" (p. 108). French became the language of administration and of the upper classes. Old English was regarded as the language of peasants. Despite this dislike of English, it continued to grow and change. It became what is called Middle English.

The following words help to illustrate the influence of Norman French on English (Funk & Funk, 1958). The Old English word for *mushroom* in English was *toad's hat* but in the 1400s the French word *moisseron* was borrowed and became *mushroom*. The word *villain* is from the French. It is originally from Latin, and meant a peasant, someone from low class, though it now means a scoundrel or criminal. The word *trespass* is from the French via the Latin word *transpassare*, which meant *pass beyond*, but now it means going beyond the limit of the law. The word *trousseau* is from the French and originally meant a little bag or sack, perhaps carried on a stick over the shoulder, that consisted of a few personal items and possibly some household linen, but it now means the clothes, linen and other belongings collected by a bride for her wedding.

For 200 years after the Norman Conquest, French was the language of the upper class and English the language of the lower class. The two languages, English and French, lived side by side for some time before they began to merge. French had social and cultural prestige and was the language of government, religion and learning. Latin was the "professional" language. It is estimated that between AD1250 and 1400, 10,000 words were adopted from Norman French and that around three-quarters are in use today. Many

English and French words have similar meanings but their connotations are somewhat different. Compare the English phrase *hearty welcome* to the French *cordial welcome*, or English *freedom* to French *liberty*.

About 200 years after the arrival of the Normans in 1066, Middle English emerged. It was a blend of the basic words of Old English and the "cultured" French the Normans had brought with them (Calfee & Patrick, 1995, p. 70). The period 1300–1500 is the Middle English period. No one is quite sure why it happened, but during this Middle English period, Old English lost its inflections. For example, the Old English spelling of "word" could be words, *worda*, *worde* or *wordum*, depending on its grammatical position. Inflectional endings disappeared from a lot of words, though some inflections stayed, like the plural -*s* and the past tense ending -*ed*.

You could say that it was all over for many Old English inflections by 1350. Why? It may have been due to the loss of status of Old English, which was regarded as the language of peasants, and this may have caused a lot of change as people no longer spoke "correct" Old English. Another possible reason was the strong emphasis on the first syllable of Old English words, so that the inflections started to get dropped off. Interference from other languages, or the criss-crossing of different dialects, may also have caused change (Bloomfield & Newmark, 1963).

The impact of the printing press and the Renaissance

In the second half of the 15th century the printing press emerged as a replacement for handwritten texts produced by scribes. While spoken English varied from region to region, written English had to be standardised. William Caxton's printing press, set up in 1475, the first to print books in English, was located next to Westminster Abbey in London, so it is not surprising that London English was recorded in print. The effect of the printing press was revolutionary. For one thing, books were so much cheaper than hand-copied manuscripts. Even Caxton's own advertisements mentioned this feature: "If it plese ony man ... to bye ... late hym come to Westmonester ... and he shal have them good chepe" (Winchester, 2003, p. 13). Caxton had a huge influence in that he used the London dialect, and he made decisions about standards of spelling as well.

The Renaissance, the revival of classical learning, saw another wave of Latin words arrive in England during the 1500s (Potter, 1966, p. 44). Although the Renaissance began much earlier than 1500 in Europe, it took time to progress to England's shores. Latin had arrived centuries before, but most of the words were linked to Christianity and the church. With the positive effect of the Renaissance on learning, many more Latin (and Greek) words and phrases came into English. For some time many words retained their original meanings. For example, *enormous* meant out of the norm, that is, abnormal, and now means very large or huge, and *extravagant* meant wandering beyond (the path), and now means going beyond reason in terms of spending money or using resources. With Latin came new prefixes (e.g., *counter-*, *dis-*, *re-*, *trans-*, *sub-*, *super-*, *pre-*, *pro-*, *de-*) and suffixes (e.g., *-able*, *-ible*, *-ent*, *-al*, *-ous* and *-ive*).

Many of the Latin words that came into the language at that time are not often used now. For example, if you saw an uncontrolled fire you would not ring the Fire Service and shout that you have just seen a *conflagration*! Although, J. K. Rowling has recently made good use of Latin words like this to give a special "magic" character to her Harry Potter books.

The Greek layer of English

As the 15th to 17th centuries passed, subject areas like science were expanding quickly and needed a lot of new words, so they borrowed many Greek words to do this, and Latin words as well. These words normally are not part of the basic vocabulary of English speakers unless they come into general use, for example, like television, which is a combination of the Greek *tele* (far) and the Latin *vision* (see). Physics, chemistry, botany, biology and medicine special terms are mostly made from Latin and Greek words. Words like *geometry*, *astronomy* and *music* are Greek. Many of the Greek and Latin words found in English today are in their original form and their meanings have remained unchanged. Many words found in science textbooks derive from Greek combining forms and Latin roots, such as *Precambrian*, *Mesozoic*, *palaeontology*, *cumulonimbus*, *amphibious*, *chlorophyll*, *mitochondria*, *anaerobic*, *hydrophobic*, *atomic*, *recalibration*, *thermosphere*, *phosphorescence*, *sedimentation*, and *archipelago*.

Summary of the French, Latin and Greek influences on English

From the time of the French-Norman invasion, through the Renaissance period, and through to 1700, the English language responded hugely and positively to change. Winchester (2003) estimates that the number of words in the language doubled from 50,000 to 100,000 by the 12th century, as a result of the French invasion, and to 200,000 by the beginning of the 17th century, as a result of the Renaissance.

Although the English language was used by great writers, such as Chaucer and Shakespeare, the language itself had very little status outside England, and this situation did not change until the 18th century and the influence of the British Empire. As a result, many scholarly works in the 1500s and 1600s were still written in Latin. Although many scholars and academics developed a love of Latin, not all did. There were many who defended English. In time many demanded that the classics be translated into English, and eventually English won over. Initially the classics were available only to those who were able to read Latin and Greek, but by 1640 more than 20,000 individual works had been published in English. The Reformation and the rise of Protestantism also contributed to the decline of Latin because of the demand for the Bible to be translated into English, and into the native languages of all the countries of Europe (Schmitt & Marsden, 2006).

The English language is a survivor. It has survived many invasions and has also been an invader itself. The colonisation of many countries around the world by the English people, including New Zealand, Australia, India, parts of South East Asia and North America, has brought many new words into the language. English in the United States, for example, has produced so many new words during its history, and has been so influential on English language speakers throughout the world, through art, writing, music, Hollywood and television, that Americans could argue, in this 21st century, that everyone is speaking American (MacNeil & Cran, 2005).

Not everyone will agree with this argument, of course, but it does illustrate that English just keeps growing in its store of words, and that words come and go, changing all the time, from expressions like Shakespeare's "whoreson beetle-headed flap-ear'd knave", which not many people currently use in their speech, to new expressions that are starting to appear in speech such as "unfriend", meaning to remove someone as a friend on your list of friends in Facebook, and "to guilt" someone, which means to make someone feel guilty.

Concluding thoughts

In teaching vocabulary, it is so important for students to understand the history of the English language: that it is not one language but is a polyglot, that it is made up of many thousands of words from many countries and that this mountain of words is a huge resource for talking, reading, listening and writing.

English is a language of invasions in that its grammar and vocabulary have been influenced by the languages of other countries. England was colonised by Iberians, Celts, Romans, Missionaries, Vikings and Danes, but it was the Old English spoken by the Anglo-Saxon tribes who paddled across the English Channel in the 5th century BC, and the French spoken by the Norman-French invasion of 1066 and the Latin and Greek vocabulary introduced by writers and scientists during the Renaissance, that were most influential in the growth of English.

This is why it is so useful to explain to students that the vocabulary of English is like a pyramid. The foundation layer of English is Anglo-Saxon.

Anglo-Saxon words are the core of English, but there are countless borrowed words. French and Latin, or the Romance layer, comprise the middle layer, and the top layer is Greek.

Thinking about English vocabulary as a pyramid helps a lot in the learning of vocabulary in that each layer has its own letter-sound correspondences for pronouncing words, its own spelling patterns and its own ways of expressing meaning. Keeping an image of the pyramid in mind will help students to grow their vocabulary, understand that for every Anglo-Saxon word there is probably a synonym from French or Latin and understand that Greek has been and still is a great source of new words for new discoveries. Thinking about the language origins of words will also help pupils to gain a better understanding of how to spell and pronounce words.

English is a growing, evolving, global language. As Winchester (2003) has put it, "Words from every corner of the globalized world cascade in ceaselessly, daily topping up a language that is self-evidently living, breathing, changing, evolving as no other language ever has, nor is ever likely to" (p. 17).

CHAPTER 2

Words: The Core Ingredient in Language

Introduction

What is a word? This chapter will explore what it means to know a word and how words are learnt. We will also review the role vocabulary plays in reading comprehension, and in writing, listening and speaking.

Vocabulary and academic progress

Everyone knows that words are the core ingredient in language. Vocabulary knowledge is important for success in reading (Gough & Tunmer, 1986; Nagy, 2007; Stahl & Nagy, 2006) and is strongly associated with success in school. The link between vocabulary knowledge and linguistic ability is very strong. What's more, word knowledge is measured to determine intelligence levels. In fact the richer a person's vocabulary, the more intelligence we attribute to them (see Anderson & Freebody, 1981, for a review; Stanovich, 2000).

Word knowledge is the core component of the *Peabody Picture Vocabulary Test: 4* (PPVT4) (Dunn & Dunn, 2007), which is administered by researchers to determine the extent of *receptive vocabulary*. The results indicate the level of verbal ability. According to Anderson and Freebody (1981, p. 77), "The strong relationship between vocabulary and general intelligence is one of the most robust findings in the history of intelligence testing." Admission into American law schools considers an extensive and rich vocabulary to be one of the most accurate indicators of potential academic and professional success. Vocabulary knowledge is necessary for effective oral and written communication, and for listening and reading comprehension.

It is all very well to talk about vocabulary and word knowledge, but how do we measure the size of someone's vocabulary? Should we measure the words that we recognise when we hear or read something (receptive vocabulary), or should we measure the words that we produce in speech or writing (productive vocabulary)? This question has challenged researchers for decades. For one thing, measuring receptive vocabulary or productive vocabulary produces different results in terms of vocabulary size. People produce fewer words in productive vocabulary than they can recognise in their receptive vocabulary. According to McCrum (1987), Shakespeare's vocabulary was about 30,000 words. However, this estimate is based on Shakespeare's productive vocabulary, and so there are many words not found in Shakespeare's writing that would probably have been in his receptive vocabulary. *Bible* and *trinity*, for example, are not found in Shakespeare's productive vocabulary (Bryson, 1991).

WORDS: THE CORE INGREDIENT IN LANGUAGE

What we do know is that competence in reading comprehension requires pupils to have an extensive vocabulary. Vocabulary knowledge is fundamental to reading comprehension. With unfamiliar words, or words not well understood, it is quite likely that pupils will attach a different meaning to them and comprehension may be affected: not necessarily overall comprehension, but precise comprehension. It is unlikely that one or two unknown words will affect the overall gist of the entire passage, but there are times when it is important to understand all the words. This is particularly evident in the complex secondary school classroom.

In the 1980s, Tom Nicholson and a team of researchers spent 18,000 minutes observing secondary students in their classrooms and conducting interviews. They found a "maze of confusion" (Nicholson, 1985, p. 515). This confusion was at all levels, from the very best readers to those experiencing reading difficulties. In one example the pupil had recorded the correct answer to a question on gravity but did not understand the concept. The researcher asked, "What's gravity?" The pupil's response was, "I don't know." The researcher continued, "What do you think gravity means? ... You must have something in your mind. What do you think it means? (long pause). Can you tell me?" The student replied, "No" (Nicholson, 1985, p. 517).

Content area reading provides many challenges for pupils. If you don't understand specific word meanings this can strongly undermine your comprehension. In content area reading the concepts are difficult, the sentences are long and complex and many students do not understand the vocabulary. Words can easily get in the way of learning. As one student explained, "You get lost when you gotta blimmin' watch the damn words" (Nicholson, 1985, p. 519).

The impact of vocabulary is direct. If a word is unknown to the reader, then the reader must rely on contextual clues. However, research suggests that readers do not often correctly infer the meaning of a word from its context (Pressley, 2000). So when comprehension at the sentence or paragraph level depends on one or two unknown words, comprehension is at risk. To put it another way, comprehension depends on word-level processing (Calfee & Drum, 1986).

Beyond the age of 10, vocabulary knowledge is critical for academic progress. Before this, students are learning to read with accuracy and fluency the thousands of words that are already part of their listening vocabulary. As children progress through school they begin to face increasingly more complex language, and if they don't know the vocabulary, their progress may well be hindered (Chall, Jacobs, & Baldwin, 1990; Pressley, 2006; Stahl & Nagy, 2006).

The word learner

Knowing the meaning of words presents a challenge for both readers and listeners. Many words have more than one meaning, words often represent abstract concepts and new definitions are added to existing words. As Labov (1973, p. 341) put it over three decades ago, "Words have often been called slippery customers, and many scholars have been distressed by their tendency to shift their word meanings and slide out from under any simple definition."

"Slippery customers" and unknown words are frequent in all types and levels of printed material, from picture books to novels. For example, imagine that the day is coming to an end and you select a picture book to read to your six-year-old. The story has two characters, Amos, a mouse, and Boris, a whale (*Amos and Boris*, Steig, 1971). This family favourite is tattered and worn, but the magic of the story is as powerful today as it was nearly two decades ago. This story about friendship contains words that are most likely outside the vocabulary of most six-year-olds:

> One night, in a phosphorescent sea, he marvelled at the sight of some whales spouting luminous water; and later, lying on the deck of his boat gazing at the immense, starry sky, the tiny mouse Amos, a little speck of a living thing in the vast living universe, felt thoroughly akin to it all. (p. 7)

In the room next door a nine-year-old is reading Morris Gleitzman's (2002) *Boy Overboard*. It is likely that this reader will also encounter unknown words. For example:

> Dad's always saying the desert's been ruined by all the abandoned tanks and crashed planes and exploded troop carriers lying around, but sometimes war debris has its uses. (p. 9)

The science material the nine-year-old was reading earlier in the evening most likely contained unknown words. The Knowing Science book, *Rudy* (Buckland, 1992), the student was reading for his research project is about cockroaches: "I'm Rudy, The Survivor, proud descendant of the pre-historic cockroaches who scrunched on earth three hundred million years ago." Other sentences provide similar vocabulary challenges: "And, clear as a bell, I heard the man call me Furtive. I have a feeling that means 'stealthy' and 'secretive'. I'll take it as a compliment." Would *descendant*, *furtive*, *stealthy*, *secretive* and *compliment* be part of a nine-year-old's vocabulary?

A young adult is reading Salman Rushdie's (2001) *Fury*. This reader is also likely to encounter words that are not well known to them, as in:

> His mother's hockey-captain grin which no shadow of pain, poverty or doubt had ever darkened and which sat so incongruously below his paternal inheritance, the beetling, dark eye-brows reminiscent of untranslatable privations endured by his ancestors in the unglamorous town of Lodz. (p. 19)

WORDS: THE CORE INGREDIENT IN LANGUAGE

How do words such as *phosphorescent*, *luminous*, *akin*, *abandoned*, *debris*, *stealthy*, *secretive*, *descendant*, *furtive*, *incongruously* and *privations* become part of our vocabulary? How many times must a reader encounter words before they are considered "known"? Just what does it mean to know a word? We turn to these questions now.

What does it mean to know a word?

This question is not easy to answer. Researchers vary in their definitions of what it means to know a word. According to Calfee and Drum (1986), knowing a word well involves:

> depth of meaning; precise usage; facile access; the ability to articulate one's understanding; flexibility in the application of the knowledge of a word; the appreciation of metaphor, analogy, word play; the ability to recognise a synonym, to define, to use a word expressively. (pp. 825–826)

Knowing a word does not occur after the reader's first encounter. Rather, vocabulary knowledge occurs in stages. Knowing a word is not simply all-or-nothing.

Beck (1979, as cited in Graves, Slater, & White, 1989) suggests there are three levels of word knowledge:

- level 1: unknown—words at this level are simply unknown
- level 2: acquainted—at this level the meaning is recognised, with deliberate attention
- level 3: established—at this level the meaning is easily, quickly and possibly automatically recognised.

Dale and O'Rourke (1986) have suggested four stages of word knowledge:

- stage 1: never saw it before
- stage 2: heard it but don't know what it means
- stage 3: recognise it in context as having something to do with …
- stage 4: know the word well.

Thus Dale and O'Rourke's stages 2 and 3 more or less expand on Beck's level 2.

As this difference indicates, it is not clear how many stages there are in knowing a word, but what we do know is that knowing a word occurs in very small incremental steps over many exposures. Consider the word *bright*. It has numerous meanings, but it takes multiple exposures to the word *bright* to acquire all these meanings. (For example, The light is bright; The future looks bright; John is bright; Sarah has a bright personality; Turn on your bright lights.)

Stahl (1983, 1985, 1986) and Stahl and Nagy (2006) suggest that knowing a word means having both definitional and contextual information about the word. Definitional information is knowledge about relationships between the word and other words. This is rather like a dictionary definition. Contextual knowledge is knowledge of a core concept and how that knowledge is applied to different contexts. For example, the word *eating* means something a little different when eating an ice-cream cone, eating an apple or eating a scrambled egg. The ice-cream is normally licked, the apple is bitten in small chunks and the scrambled egg is eaten with the aid of a utensil (see Stahl & Fairbanks, 1986, p. 74).

Levels of word knowledge, or how well a word is known, can become apparent in specific contexts. In some contexts we seem to know a word well, but in other contexts we do not. For example, it is possible that we know the word *earthquake* in the everyday sense, but when chatting to a seismologist our understanding of the word may prove to be somewhat elementary. Likewise we may consider that our understanding of the word *language* is good until we are introduced to Noam Chomsky.

The first time an unknown word is encountered the reader has several options. One option is to skip the word. When encountering the occasional unknown word readers will skip it if it does not affect the overall gist of the passage. The reader, however, does store away one or more aspects of the word. That is, something about the word is remembered. It may be its spelling pattern or the context in which the word occurred. The reader may also search for familiar word patterns, such as known prefixes or word roots. After each encounter with the word the reader stores away more information until such time as the word is known. Multiple exposures to a word are critical if the word is to become part of the reader's vocabulary.

Word knowledge grows at a fairly constant rate provided the reader is exposed to print. It is rather like a jigsaw. One piece of the puzzle does not result in a completed puzzle. Over time piece after piece are connected, and eventually the puzzle is completed. Likewise, our first encounter with a word does not result in knowing the word. However, with each encounter we store away in memory more information about the word until the word is known.

The reader faces a number of obstacles to increasing their vocabulary. Consider, for a start, the fact that many words are polysemous (have many meanings). Take the word *ring*. The following meanings do resemble one another but they are not identical:

- John gave Sarah an engagement ring.
- The boxer entered the ring well prepared for the fight.
- Please put a ring around 26 June.
- Alex replaced three ring-binders.

WORDS: THE CORE INGREDIENT IN LANGUAGE

What does it mean to know the word *ring*? It means understanding its core meaning, but it also means having the ability to use the word flexibly. It means knowing the subtle changes in meaning between contexts. Not only does the reader need to know the dictionary definition, including synonyms and antonyms, but they also need contextual knowledge (Nagy, 2007; Stahl, 1983, 1985, 1986).

How many encounters before a word is known? McKeown, Beck, Omanson, and Pople (1985) found that reading comprehension was improved after 12 encounters with a word. However, 12 encounters does not necessarily mean that the word is known well. Nagy and Scott (2000) report that after 40 encounters with a word students have yet to reach a ceiling.

Carey and Bartlett (1978) carried out a simple experiment with three-year-old children. The children did not know the colour olive. Some children called olive brown and others referred to it as green. The authors found that a week after the pupils encountered the new word for olive they remembered that olive was not brown or green. They did not remember the new word, but they knew what it wasn't; nor did they use green or brown.

Word learners are quick at recognising a new word. Words are then assigned to semantic categories (colour category, flower category, animal category, etc.). The next stage takes time. Indeed, for some words the next stage of learning the subtle or not-so-subtle differences between words never eventuates. The challenge word learners face is being able to be specific about words. For example, the word learner may know that a camellia and an azalea are both shrubs. The next stage is to distinguish one from the other when seen. Young New Zealanders may know that tui, kakapo and saddleback belong to the field of New Zealand native birds. The next stage would be being able to identify the birds in the bush.

Beck, McKeown, and Omanson (1987) (refer also to Beck & McKeown, 2007; Beck, McKeown, & Kucan, 2002) suggest there are three tiers of vocabulary knowledge (as opposed to the stages or degrees of learning we looked at above). The first tier consists of basic everyday words. Words such as *cat*, *dog*, *mother*, *father*, *chair*, *table*, *grass* and so on are located in tier one. According to Beck et al. (1987), these words do not need to form part of the instructional word study programme for native English speakers because they are well known to the reader. The second tier consists of nonbasic words of high frequency. They are considered generalist words rather than words associated with a specific field (rather like the generalist knowledge a general practitioner requires compared to the specialist knowledge required of an ear, nose and throat doctor or a cardiologist). Instruction in tier three words is best left to when the specific need arises. Instead, instruction should focus on words in the second tier. Second-tier words include *diligent*, *influential*, *procrastinate*, *distinguish*, *frequency*, *scavenger* and *unique*. Knowledge of these relatively high-frequency words is necessary for general comprehension. The third tier consists of words with low frequency levels. These words are often associated with specific knowledge domains such as chemistry, biology, aviation or agriculture. Words such as *photoperiodism* (the cycles of plants in temperate climates), *transgenesis* (using genetic engineering techniques), *gravimetric* (weighing substances) and *aviatrix* (female aviator) belong to this third tier. Words in this third tier rarely occur in printed English, and knowledge of these words is not necessary for mature language users.

In summary, research shows that word learning is incremental. With each encounter with a word our knowledge about the word grows. The steps in knowing a word are very small. To know a word well requires many encounters in meaningful contexts. Part 2 of this book will outline practical strategies teachers can use to help their students develop more knowledge about words.

The role of vocabulary in reading comprehension

We have already noted in a general way the importance of vocabulary to reading comprehension, and the importance of reading comprehension to academic progress. In this section we will look in more detail at these connections.

According to the National Reading Panel (2000, p. 4-1):

> Comprehension is critically important to the development of children's reading skills and therefore their ability to obtain an education. Indeed, reading comprehension has come to be viewed as the 'essence of reading', essential not only to academic learning but to life-long learning.

But what is reading comprehension? To define reading comprehension would be to define reading, and this is very complex. Comprehension is associated with understanding and meaning. It is where the "meanings of words are integrated into sentences and text structures" (Juel, 1988, p. 438). Or, put another way, it is 'the process by which, given lexical (i.e., word) information, sentences and discourses are interpreted' (Gough & Tunmer, 1986, p. 7).

Reading comprehension is the ability to comprehend written language. Skilled reading requires skill in both decoding and comprehension (Gough & Tunmer, 1986). According to the simple view of reading (Gough & Tunmer, 1986), the reader is one who is able to decode and comprehend the text. This includes understanding the text at the word level. Calfee and Drum (1986) have identified four components of reading comprehension, and vocabulary is one of these. Without vocabulary knowledge, reading comprehension would not occur.

WORDS: THE CORE INGREDIENT IN LANGUAGE

Dymock and Nicholson (2007) argue that reading comprehension occurs over several stages (see Figure 2.1). In order to comprehend written text, the reader must first decode the print. Next the reader looks up the words in their mental dictionary (or lexicon), after which they analyse the sentence to gain understanding. The reader must then grasp the main idea of each paragraph. Finally, they must understand the text as a whole.

FIGURE 2.1: THE STAGES OF READING COMPREHENSION

Decoding the printed message → Vocabulary lookup in the mental lexicon → Sentence parsing and analysis → Paragraph interpretation → Text structure analysis

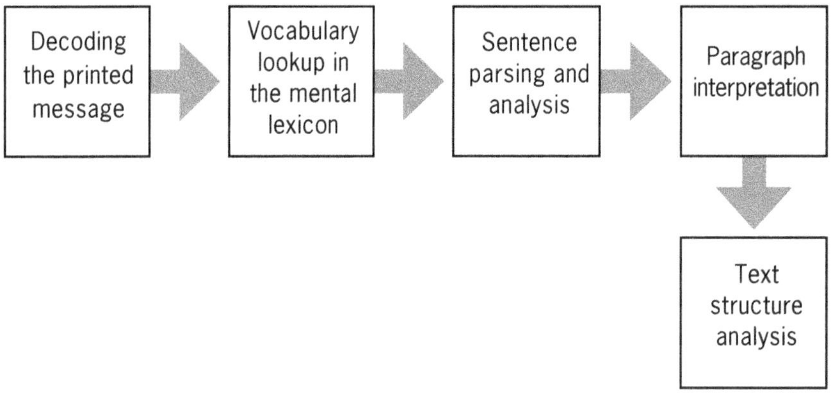

Gough and Tunmer's (1986) simple view of reading includes only two components: decoding and linguistic comprehension. Decoding includes fluency and accuracy, while linguistic comprehension subsumes levels of vocabulary knowledge. The National Reading Panel (2000) has identified five essential components that are critical for reading success. They include the three subcomponents of decoding (phonemic awareness, phonics and fluency), vocabulary and text comprehension.

Knowledge of word meanings is critical to reading comprehension. Nagy and Herman (1987, p. 27) put it simply: "Children who know more words understand text better." As a result, the number of words a reader knows provides a relatively accurate prediction of their ability to comprehend the text. Readers with large vocabularies will encounter fewer challenges when comprehending a story than readers with small vocabularies. As children progress through school they encounter more complex text. Text normally associated with content area reading places a high demand on vocabulary knowledge. Imagine a 15-year-old student preparing for a test on earthquakes. If the student has an understanding of words and phrases such as *tectonic plate*, *fault line*, *seismic waves*, *tremors*, *tsunamis*, *seismometer*, *seismograph*, *epicentre*, *magnitude*, *energy* and *Richter Scale*, then it is quite likely the test would not present any great challenges. However, if the words are unknown or are "blimmin' getting in the way", comprehension is at risk—as well as success in the test.

As Nagy (1988, p. 1) puts it:

> Vocabulary knowledge is fundamental to reading comprehension; one cannot understand text without knowing what most of the words mean. A wealth of research has documented the strength of the relationship between vocabulary and comprehension. The proportion of difficult words in a text is the single most powerful predictor of text difficulty, and a reader's general vocabulary knowledge is the single best predictor of how well that reader can understand text.

Overall, then, there is little debate over the importance of vocabulary in reading comprehension. In outlining the sources of comprehension failure, Perfetti, Marron, and Foltz (1996) list "word meanings" as one. They state, "The role of vocabulary [in reading comprehension failure] is obvious enough. A failure to understand words in text will cause problems in understanding the text" (p. 142).

How many words does the reader need to know? Nagy and Scott (2000) estimate that the reader needs to know the meaning of 90–95 percent of the words in the text for adequate comprehension. If a reader knows 90 percent of the words, they are able to use this knowledge to learn the remaining 10 percent. If the reader knows less than 90 percent of the words, comprehension is at risk. What's more, the reader will have lost an opportunity to add to their lexicon. In other words, the reader is affected by a double whammy: they lose the opportunity to gain content knowledge *and* to add to their vocabulary.

For over eight decades researchers have acknowledged the strong relationship between vocabulary and reading comprehension (Thorndike, 1917), but it seems clear this relationship is causal. As Stanovich (2000, p. 182) puts it, "variation in vocabulary knowledge is a causal determinant of differences in reading comprehension ability". It is possible to tease out further how this causal relationship works. Anderson and Freebody (1981) suggest three possibilities. The first is the instrumentalist hypothesis, which suggests that vocabulary knowledge enables the reader or listener to understand/comprehend. Hypothesis two (general aptitude) and hypothesis three (general knowledge) suggest that vocabulary knowledge and reading comprehension are related to knowledge of the world. According to Hirsch (2003, p. 10), "reading comprehension requires knowledge of the words and the world".

The role of vocabulary in listening and speaking

Although the focus of this book is on vocabulary and reading it is important to acknowledge the critical role vocabulary plays in listening and speaking. Listening comprehension is "at risk" if the listener does not know what the word/s mean. Senechal, Ouellette, and Rodney (2006, p. 177) refer to the "predictive role of vocabulary knowledge to listening comprehension". In other words, vocabulary size is an indicator of listening comprehension. Children with smaller vocabularies will comprehend less. Children with a large vocabulary will comprehend more. Hart and Risley (2003) also acknowledge the critical role vocabulary plays in understanding. They found that vocabulary growth rates are strongly associated with cognitive growth rates.

The ability to follow directions, understand verbal instructions, comprehend oral text (e.g., radio, listening to the teacher read) partly depends on listening vocabulary. Receptive vocabulary (i.e., listening vocabulary) is used as a measure of verbal ability. According to Sternberg (1987) vocabulary knowledge is probably the best indicator of an individual's verbal ability. A small listening vocabulary is a huge obstacle. A Year 4 class listening to their teacher talk about a wedding they attended over the weekend (e.g., *toast* the bride, *groom*, *vow*) will be cut out of part of the conversation if they do not know the meaning of *toast*, *groom* and *vow*.

Students are also "at risk" if they do not have the vocabulary to express themselves. Without adequate vocabulary they may not be able to communicate clearly or precisely with their teacher, friends, parents, their doctor and, in time, their employer. Without adequate vocabulary communication breakdown can easily occur.

What influences children's vocabulary levels?

A possible explanation for individual differences in children's vocabulary on entry to school is the amount of exposure to language that different children have, either through verbal interaction and listening to books read to them by their caregivers, or through other sources like television. The relationship between vocabulary and success in school is so profound and intricately linked that Hart and Risley (2003) refer to young children with relatively low vocabularies as "the early catastrophe" (p. 4).

Hart and Risley (1995) have shown that at school entry some children will know twice as many words as their classmates, and that as they progress through school this difference increases. Why does the gap in vocabulary, and in turn comprehension, increase? There are rich get richer effects in vocabulary learning in that the more words children have in their vocabulary the easier it is to learn new words because they have more knowledge to draw on. Likewise, there are poor get poorer effects in that the fewer words in their vocabulary, the fewer new words they will learn.

For example, imagine a group of 15-year-old students in a science class who have a science text to read. According to Nagy and Scott (2000), reading comprehension depends on knowing what the words mean and, as we have seen, they estimate that to comprehend a text readers must know between 90 and 95 percent of the words. Students with a good science vocabulary will comprehend the assigned chapter. Those who do not know the meaning of 90 percent or more of the words will not. Readers who know a lot of words will not only add words to their mental lexicon but will learn from the content they read as well. In other words, the rich get richer (Stanovich, 1986). Readers with a smaller vocabulary will experience difficulties comprehending not only what they read but also what they hear—and they will also acquire fewer new words than will readers with a larger vocabulary. A smaller vocabulary will in turn negatively affect their ability to communicate ideas in speaking and writing, compared with readers who have a larger vocabulary. These rich get richer and poor get poorer effects are called Matthew effects (Stanovich, 2000).

How can teachers go about bridging this gap between the vocabulary rich and the vocabulary poor? Blachowicz and Fisher (2000) and Stahl and Nagy (2006) suggest that some form of instruction is better than leaving vocabulary gains to incidental learning. In other words, the teacher can, and should, play an important role in vocabulary acquisition. This does not mean we should jump straight into teaching tier 3 words like *stegosaur* and *lachrymose*, because Biemiller and Slonim (2001) have shown that children learn words in a particular order.

Biemiller and Slonim's (2001) findings suggest that root words are generally learnt in the same order by most children. They also report that by the end of Grade 2 (or eight to nine years) children making grade-appropriate progress will understand most Level 2 words, half of Level 4 words and a third of Level 6 words from Dale and O'Rourke's (1981) *Living Word Vocabulary*. The *Living Word Vocabulary* outlines an order of word learning. This list is not *exact*, rather an indication based on Dale and O'Rourke's (1981) research over two decades.

Biemiller (2005, p. 232) states, "The existence of a strong order in which words are acquired means that 'individual differences' are, in fact, mainly 'developmental differences' in that some words are harder to learn than others and require more maturity and depth of knowledge and vocabulary to come to grips with their meanings." This makes sense in that we are much more likely to hear five-year-olds use words like *cat* rather than *feline* when describing their family pet, and they are much more likely to say *old* than *anachronistic* when describing the age of their parents. So in teaching, we are better off to focus on tier 2 words that pupils are going to find easier to learn. How best to do that is covered in later chapters.

WORDS: THE CORE INGREDIENT IN LANGUAGE

Summary

This chapter has explored what it means to know a word, and how words are learnt. The chapter has also examined the crucial role that vocabulary plays in understanding what we read, as well as its importance in writing, listening and speaking. Whether we are producing vocabulary, as in speaking and writing, or comprehending vocabulary, as in reading and listening, our comprehension is completely dependent on knowing what words mean (Samuels, 1987).

The take home messages of this chapter are:

- Not all children start school knowing the same number of words—some know lot more words than others.
- Not all words are equally easy to learn, in that some words take more time and knowledge to get under our belts.
- There are positive Matthew effects in learning new words in that the more words you already know, the easier it is to learn new words.
- Exposure to language, through listening and interacting with others, especially caregivers, and through listening to stories, and reading stories yourself, is a great way to learn new words.
- Teachers can help their class to learn new words but have to adjust teacher language to the language of the class, so as to connect new words to the words their class already know.
- It is better to teach tier 2 words (primary school) before tier 3 words (high school); that is, try not to teach words like *graminivorous* (eating grass) and *lugubrious* (melancholy, mournful) to five-year-olds, at least not until the class has a grip on tier 1 basic words that will connect to these unfamiliar words, like *grass* and *sad*.

Fortunately, most writers of children's stories and books are aware that there are tiers of words, so that teachers can ensure children are on the right track by organising for them to read text material that is written for their age level, and by talking with them a lot and listening to the words they use, so the teacher can connect the words their pupils know already to the learning of new words.

When is a good time to be learning tier 2 words? The answer is any time at all. Even at Year 1 of school, children will already be learning lots of tier 2 words (for example, *pyramid* when they study "the food pyramid"), and they will be writing sentences in their writing books made up from discussion with the teacher, such as "The food pyramid looks like a triangle. It has got six parts. It helps us to eat a variety of foods to keep us healthy." Their sentences will have what are possibly unfamiliar words, like *pyramid*, *triangle* and *variety*.

This is great—even five-year-olds can be learning lots of new words from their first weeks and months at school.

The trick is for the teacher to use strategies to help their students understand what these tier 2 words mean, and we will be discussing some "tricks", that is, strategies, that the teacher can use when we look at the teaching of vocabulary in the following chapters.

CHAPTER 3

Catering for Diverse Learners

Introduction

So far we have been focusing on vocabulary acquisition in English-language speakers. However, many children do not have English as their first language, and it seems likely that they, and their teachers, will face specific challenges when it comes to developing their vocabulary. This chapter looks at how we might go about catering for the diverse array of learners encountered in today's schools.

Learning English as an additional language

The number of students learning English as an additional language in many English-speaking countries has grown exponentially during the past two decades and will continue to grow. In 1979 there were six million students in the United States learning English as an additional language, and in 1999 there were 14 million (August & Shanahan, 2006). Garcia (2003) reports that approximately 22 percent of US school-age children live in homes where English is not their first language. In the state of California, 50 percent of students speak English as an additional language, and it is estimated that by 2030 this will rise to 70 percent (Fitzgerald, 1995).

There are also a significant number of children living in New Zealand who are learning English as an additional language. In one primary school in a middle-sized New Zealand city, 178 students (27 percent of the total school roll) are learning English as an additional language (B. Cowie, personal communication, 27 November 2009). This is quite a different picture from 1989, when only a few students in New Zealand primary and intermediate classrooms were learning English as a second language. In some classrooms students learning English as an additional language may in fact be the majority rather than the minority.

According to Graves (2006, p. 86) there are four significant challenges facing English-language learners:
- developing a basic vocabulary of the most frequent words in English
- building a vocabulary of academic English (particularly for students wanting to study at an advanced level)
- understanding the thousands of idioms in English (e.g., *break a leg* and *to have the upper hand*)
- realising that some English words may also represent new concepts for the student, so not only are they learning a new word but a new concept as well.

There is little debate that a limited vocabulary is a huge barrier when speaking, listening, writing and reading. Considerable research suggests that poor reading comprehension for English-language learners is partly due to low vocabulary (Garcia, 1991; Helman, 2009; Nagy, 1997; Snow, Burns, & Griffin, 1998). Because vocabulary plays such a critical role in comprehension, the reading achievement gap between good and poor readers in New Zealand (see Progress in International Reading Literacy Study, Mullis, Martin, Kennedy, & Foy, 2007) could *partly* be attributed to the limited vocabulary of English-language learners. As we have seen in previous chapters, a low or limited vocabulary has a negative impact on decoding and comprehension.

As second-language learners progress through primary school they face an increasing number of academic words. Due to their often surface understanding of vocabulary, comprehension is at risk. These readers also lack familiarity with the less common word meanings. For example, English-language learners might know that *terminal* means a building at the airport but may not know that *terminal* also means someone undergoing the last stage of a fatal disease or "a point of connection in an electric circuit or device" (Deverson, 1998, p. 844). English-language learners might know that *small* means not big or large, but may become confused when reference is made to *small talk*, *small hours* or *small change*.

What do teachers need to know in order to provide an effective classroom programme for students who are learning English as an additional language? Paul Nation (1990, p. 4) identifies three points teachers should consider when developing a vocabulary programme for English-language users: the vocabulary students need to know, how students will learn the vocabulary (e.g., explicit teaching, exposure to language) and how to assess whether the students know the vocabulary they need to know or have learnt the vocabulary the teacher considers they need to know.

Which words do English-language learners need to learn?

In this context Nation (1990) and others (e.g., Coelho, 2004) suggest that vocabulary can be separated into three general groups:
- high-frequency words
- low-frequency words
- specialised words (i.e., academic and technical vocabulary).

The attentive reader will recall that we used a similar division in Chapter 2, involving three tiers of words (see Beck & McKeown, 2007). However, there we were discussing native English speakers as opposed to English-language learners. We will discuss the relationship between the three tiers and the above-mentioned frequency groups shortly.

High-frequency words

High-frequency or everyday words are words that speakers, listeners, readers and writers use to get by in their daily lives. About half are from the Anglo-Saxon layer of English and half are from Latin, French or Greek (Nation, 1990). High-frequency words include common nouns (e.g., *house, car, bed, drink, teacher, store, work, bus, doctor*), verbs (e.g., *eat, sleep, walk, drink*) and function words (e.g., *the, but*), and they are fundamental to receptive and productive English. About 80 percent of words in text are high-frequency words (Nation, 2001, p. 11).

Where can teachers access these high-frequency words? West (1953) created a list of 2,000 high-frequency "head" words known as the General Service List. (The list can be retrieved from http://jbauman.com/gsl.html.) The General Service List consists of words that are considered to be of "general service" to English-language learners. In 1995 John Bauman and Brent Culligan updated the General Service List, and the list now contains 2,284 words. (The updated General Service List can be downloaded from http://jbauman.com/aboutgsl.html.) There are also a number of other lists (see Nation, 1990, for a short summary of lists, including their strengths and weaknesses). Carroll, Davies, and Richman (1971) have also produced a list of over 80,000 words, in order of frequency. This large corpus represents printed American school English for Grades 3–9 (ages 9–15).

Having an understanding of high-frequency words is critical to success in oral and written language. Although English-language learners face a huge challenge, it is not insurmountable. One word alone—*the*—accounts for 6–7 percent of words in a passage and is the most frequent word in connected text (Carroll et al., 1971; Nation, 2005). Nation (2005) reports that the 10 most frequent English words account for 25 percent of words in connected text, the 100 most frequent words account for 50 percent and the 1,000 most frequent words account for 70–80 percent. High-frequency words form the foundation for basic English and they need to be learnt.

Low-frequency words

The next phase in learning English is low-frequency words. Low-frequency words are the largest group of words. Nation (1990) estimates there are about 123,000 low-frequency words, which can be grouped into four types (Nation, 2001). The first group are considered "moderately frequent" but have not made it to the high-frequency list. They are "boundary words"—on the boundary between high- and low-frequency words. *Curious*, for example, is on the low-frequency list. The second group of low-frequency words are the proper nouns (e.g., *St Lucia, Waitangi, Wellington, Mt Cook*). The third group may be considered low-frequency to some but not others. For example, cricketers or rowers or vulcanologists will have a group of words that are considered high-frequency to them but low-frequency to others. The fourth group of low-frequency words are of very low frequency. These are words English-language users rarely use (e.g., *plummet, ploy, bifurcate*).

Specialised words

Specialised words can be separated into two groups: academic and technical. There are about 800 *academic* words (Nation, 1990), and these words occur frequently in academic texts (e.g., *integrate, emphasise, contrast, correspond, compare, participate, accumulate*). Specialised words are important for high school and tertiary students and should be introduced to senior primary and intermediate students. About 8 percent of words in academic texts are considered academic words (Nation, 1990).

Approximately 3 percent of words in specialised texts are *technical* vocabulary (Nation, 1990). The majority of these words are from the Latin/French and Greek layers of English (see Chapter 1). For example, learning about economics means learning the vocabulary associated with economics (e.g., *market, economy, goods, scarcity, demand, price-effect*). Learning about maths means learning the vocabulary associated with the subject (e.g., *diameter, circumference, metre, divide, multiply, fraction, length, capacity*). Learning about insects means learning the vocabulary associated with insects (e.g., *thorax, exoskeleton, cocoon, larva, antennae, abdomen*). Nation (1990) claims there are about 1,000–2,000 technical words for any subject. Content area reading requires an understanding of technical (or subject-specific) vocabulary.

Working with words of different frequencies

How can teachers identify high-frequency, low-frequency, academic and technical words in a text? Lexical Tutor, a computer program available free on http://www.lextutor.ca/, identifies word types. Teachers can either enter or copy and paste text into Lexical Tutor. Once you have accessed the programme, click on Vocabprofile (under RESEARCH heading), then click on Classic VP English v.3 and enter your text. After entering the text press 'SUBMIT'. The first 1,000 words from the General Service list will appear in blue, and the second 1,000 in green. Academic words are in yellow and off-list words are in red.

In the *School Journal* article "Plants that Store Water" (Shannon, 1993), written at the 8.5–9.5 age level, 85 percent of the total running words are from the first 1,000 words, 6 percent are from the second 1,000, there are no academic words and 8 percent are off-list words. It is not surprising that an article written at the 8.5–9.5 age level contains no academic words. Off-list words are the technical words associated with the subject, such as *cacti* and *succulents* (see words in bold below). To comprehend "Plants that Store Water", students would need some understanding of the words *cactus/cacti*, *succulents* and *spines*—technical words associated with the article.

The following is an extract from "Plants that Store Water" (pp. 11–12). The first 1,000 words from the General Service List are in regular font, the second 1,000 are in italics and words not on the list are in bold.

> When I was little, I kept **cactus** plants. I like their **weird** shapes and **spines**, and found they were very easy to grow. I'm not very good at remembering to water *pot* plants, but my **cacti** didn't seem to mind if I forgot occasionally.
>
> Like all plants, **cacti** need water. But **cacti** belong to a special group of plants (called '**succulents**') that are able to do without water for longer than most. This is because **succulents** are able to store water.
>
> **Cacti** store water in their stems. (The 'leaves' are needles.) Other **succulents**, like this plant, store water in their leaves.
>
> **Succulents** live in many places where there isn't much water. For example, they grow high in the mountains where water often *freezes*. They grow near the sea where the water is too salty to use. The most famous **succulents**, the **cacti**, usually grow in deserts where it is very hot and dry *during* the day, and cold at night.
>
> **Cacti** must protect themselves from the hot sun. When the sun is **overhead**, it could easily *damage* the *delicate* growing point at the top of the plant. So most **cacti** have *lots* of **spines** at the top which give *shade* like an *umbrell*a. Some **cacti** produce a kind of *wool* instead of **spines**.
>
> This *wool* protects the plant from the sun, and it will also keep it *warm during* the cold nights.

"Swimming: Then and Now" (Duder, 1995), a more advanced text than "Plants that Store Water" written for Years 7–8 students, has a different profile from "Plants that Store Water". While the majority of the words are from the first 1,000-word list (i.e., 77 percent), 9 percent are from the second, 3 percent from the academic word list and 12 percent are off-list words. Academic words in "Swimming: Then and Now" include *author, apparently, designed, creating, energy, technique, available, experts, methods, psychologists, visualise* and *individual*. As texts increase in difficulty the percentage of academic and off-list words increases. Off-list words in "Swimming: Then and Now" include *Tessa Duder, Cardiff, Wales, Alex, Pamela, squad, lane, medal, Commonwealth, swimmer, coaches, heartbeat, champions, squad, togs, nylons, goggles, chlorine*; these include proper nouns (low frequency) and technical words (specialised words). Lexical Tutor is particularly useful for identifying words that may be appropriate to pre-teach before reading a text.

What is the relationship between Beck and McKeown's (2007) "tiers of words" discussed in Chapter 2 and the words on the General Service List and academic and technical words? Basically, Beck and McKeown's tiers relate to native English speakers. Tier one words are common sight words and simple nouns and verbs. Tier two words are often from the Latin layer of English. Tier three words are rare (subject-specific words, such as *thorax*). Native English speakers are familiar with tier one words. Although there are some exceptions, generally the first 2,000 words on the General Service List are in tier one (M. McKeown, personal communication, 12 December 2009). Non-native English-language learners are not familiar with tier one words. Tier two words (academic words) are generally unfamiliar to all students, so all students would benefit from being taught tier two or academic words. Tier three words (or technical words) are considered rare and should be taught in conjunction with content area and topic reading.

We have established the types of words English-language learners need to learn. The next section will show how to meet this challenge, and recommends the best conditions for learning English vocabulary, including ideas on how to foster the relationship between vocabulary learning in two languages. In Part 2 of this book we will go on to give practical exercises for teaching vocabulary.

Meeting the challenge of teaching students vocabulary

According to Coelho (2004), English-language learners, when learning in an English-language setting, take about five years to reach the same level of academic language proficiency as their peers. Fitzgerald (1995, p. 118) suggests that up to eight years may be needed for English-language learners to learn formal academic language, including the ability to comprehend complex text. This is achieved only as a result of a planned and deliberately taught programme. It is possible that some learners may never reach the proficiency of their peers.

Table 3.1 identifies six developmental stages of oral vocabulary (Coelho, 2004). Stage 1 represents students who are new to English. These students have no understanding of English vocabulary. Students at stage 2 are beginning to use functional vocabulary (e.g., words associated with food, clothing and classroom objects such as *desk, chair, door, room, pencil, paper, book* etc). Knowing what stage the student is at will enable the teacher to plan an appropriate programme. It is quite possible that classrooms will have students at a number of developmental stages.

TABLE 3.1: DEVELOPMENTAL STAGES IN ORAL COMMUNICATION IN ENGLISH

	STAGE 1	STAGE 2	STAGE 3	STAGE 4	STAGE 5	STAGE 6
Vocabulary	New to English	Uses functional vocabulary	Uses limited vocabulary	Uses adequate vocabulary; some word-usage irregularities	Uses varied vocabulary	Uses extensive vocabulary but may lag behind native-speaking peers

Source: Coelho, 2004, p. 253

Helman (2009) reviewed a number of vocabulary interventions for English-language learners and, as a result, established a number of guiding principles for teachers:

1. Instruction should build on what students know.
2. Instruction should address the learning needs of the student. Some students may be at stage 2, others at stage 4, so developing a single programme for all English-language learners may save time for the teacher but will not be beneficial to the student. A stage 2 student and a stage 4 student have very different learning needs, and the classroom programme should reflect this.
3. Vocabulary instruction should be taught in meaningful contexts. Research indicates that vocabulary is enhanced if instruction occurs in context and students have many opportunities to use and apply new vocabulary. [Note: Stahl and Fairbanks' (1986) meta-analysis found that the most effective vocabulary teaching included definition and context information and when students had multiple exposures to the target words.]
4. Instruction must be comprehensive and in depth—looking up a word in the dictionary is not considered in depth or comprehensive.
5. Teachers should not only develop a programme but commit themselves to implementing it.

Assessing vocabulary

Assessment is fundamental to knowing what to teach. Knowing the vocabulary stage the student is at (see Table 3.1) enables teachers to plan an appropriate programme. Assessing vocabulary, however, presents a challenge to teachers. Standardised vocabulary measures such as the *Peabody Picture Vocabulary Test: 4* (PPVT-4) (Dunn & Dunn, 2007) may disadvantage linguistically and culturally diverse students because the vocabulary and experiences the measure is based on may be foreign to them. Both the vocabulary subcomponents of *Progressive Achievement Test: Reading* (Darr, McDowall, Ferral, Twist, & Watson, 2008) and *STAR: Supplementary Test of Achievement in Reading: Years 4–6* and *Years 7–9* (Elley, 2000, 2001) assess reading vocabulary. Scores for students experiencing decoding difficulties will not necessarily be an accurate indication of their vocabulary level. The *Progressive Achievement Test: Reading* and *STAR: Supplementary Test of Achievement in Reading: Years 4–6* and *Years 7–9* are both written tests. Students experiencing decoding difficulties face challenges accessing printed text and this negatively affects written vocabulary test scores. For example, a student might know the meaning of *volcanologists* but due to decoding difficulties is unable to decode *volcanologists* so scores this question wrong on the test. If the word was presented orally, and decoding skills were not required, the student would get the question correct. In other words, written text scores may not be an accurate indication of vocabulary levels for students experiencing decoding difficulties.

Consideration must be given to assessing receptive vocabulary (listening, reading), productive vocabulary (speaking, writing) or both. New learners of English may have a higher listening and reading vocabulary than a speaking or writing vocabulary, so assessing receptive vocabulary will not necessarily give an indication of productive vocabulary. We suggest teachers begin by assessing students' oral proficiency (listening and speaking), then their reading comprehension and finally their writing.

For students who have had no exposure to English, assessment is unnecessary. For students who have had some exposure, we recommend teachers begin by informally assessing their oral vocabulary. Start by having a social conversation with the student. Ask their name and/or how they like to spend their free time. If the student is able to answer one or two simple questions, continue with the conversation. Note or record their vocabulary. Walk around the classroom and playground saying the names of concrete objects (e.g., chair, tree, leaves, pencil, book) and ask the student to point to the objects. Or have a selection of pictures of concrete objects, say the name of the object and then have the student point to the picture or object (similar to the *Peabody Picture Vocabulary Test–4*, Dunn & Dunn, 2007).

Another informal measure that can be used to assess receptive vocabulary is to have the student follow oral instructions (e.g., "Can you get the pen from my desk" or "Please put this book in the library corner"), or observe students when giving group or whole-class instructions. Note whether the student initiates conversation. Students can also orally retell a story or article they have heard. Material should be selected carefully to ensure students have some content knowledge. *Journal Surf*, an online catalogue of the *School Journal*, enables teachers to search under topics as well as readability level. *Journal Surf* is managed by Learning Media, the publishing arm of the Ministry of Education. There is an annual subscription fee and most schools subscribe (http://journalsurf.learningmedia.co.nz/).

A more formal measure of vocabulary is to select words from the General Service List (the first 1,000, then the second 1,000). Ask students to place a tick next to the words they know. Self-reporting measures are problematic, however, because students may not be clear on what it means to know a word, or they may tick words they do not know. Cunningham and Stanovich (1990) developed the Title Recognition Test as a way of measuring print exposure. Students are given a list of book titles and asked to tick the books they have read or listened to. To prevent children ticking titles of books they have not read, foils are interspersed among the actual titles. Foils could also be interspersed among the sample from the General Service List (e.g., nonwords such as *dit*, *gaction*).

More advanced English-language learners could take Nation's (1990, pp. 261–272) Vocabulary Levels Test, or part of the test. The test is organised into five levels, from the first 2,000 words on the General Service List (Level 1) to the 10,000-word list that contains advanced words (e.g, *dabble*, *pompous*, *seclusion*). A sample of Level 1 follows. Instructions begin with:

> This is a vocabulary test. You must choose the right word to go with each meaning. Write the number of that word next to its meaning.
>
> 1. business
> 2. clock
> 3. horse   _____ part of a house
> 4. pencil   _____ animal with four legs
> 5. shoe   _____ something used for writing
> 6. wall

Sentence and paragraph comprehension can be assessed using "cloze" procedure. Cloze procedure (or "testing") is when words are deleted from a passage and students are asked to replace the words using context from the remaining words. The extent that students can replace the words is an indication of comprehension. Cloze procedure draws on the students' word knowledge. To complete the activity, students must have an understanding of what the words mean. Two types of cloze passages would be suitable for English-language learners. One is where students complete the sentence without a list of possible words to select from; for example, "Today the _____ is shining. I ate an _____ for lunch." The other is where students select the most appropriate words from a list, thus providing more support for the student; for example, "Select the best word from the following list: *dog, jar, desk, book*. I took my _____ for a walk." When developing a cloze exercise, select subjects the student will have some knowledge of (e.g., do not have a passage about snowboarding if the student comes from Africa, or a passage about junk food if the student comes from China).

Written vocabulary should be assessed if the student is able to complete a reading assessment. Students can write, in list form, words they know. Alternatively, students can write a story, letter or diary entry.

Vocabulary instruction and resources that support vocabulary development

Hawkins (2005, p. 30) reports that there is little empirical research on "English language learning and teaching in elementary [primary] schools". What we do know is that vocabulary knowledge is fundamental to success in school.

As put by Wong Fillmore (cited in Hawkins, 2005, p. 31):
> what all students, including ELLs [English-language learners], must have to deal with the new expectations (curriculum and assessment reforms, benchmark testing etc.) is a mature understanding of the English used in texts and academic settings.

Helman's (2009) review of a number of studies aimed at increasing vocabulary found that interventions that resulted in increased vocabulary:

- presented words in meaningful contexts rather than in isolation
- used lessons that encouraged and motivated students
- involved in-depth and long-term interventions that featured repetition and review
- used discussions around the text
- involved vocabulary study/lessons that built on students' main language
- taught strategies for learning words
- provided support (e.g., through the use of visuals, practise in oral language).

There is considerable research to support the importance of a language-rich classroom for vocabulary development. Classroom teachers must also give careful consideration to which vocabulary to teach and the importance of teaching/developing word-learning strategies. The following ideas will help foster vocabulary development for students learning English as an additional language as well as native English speakers.

Oral-rich classrooms

English-language learners need regular opportunities to talk. Such opportunities do not just happen: they require planning. Organised talk can be one to one or in small groups. Students should be encouraged to tell stories, including experiences of their home country.

Visual-rich classrooms

Recently published material that includes pictures to illustrate concepts and words should be visible and easily accessible to students (e.g., illustrated encyclopaedias and dictionaries, picture books that label objects). Colourful charts and posters that label common mathematical concepts (e.g., *square, circle, metre, centimetre, time*), vocabulary associated with current unit topics (e.g., *mammals, insects, solar system*), parts of the body and parts of the home and classroom should be seen, read and discussed.

Print-rich classrooms

For many students the classroom is their main source of books. A weekly 30-minute visit to the school library is important, but the visit should not be a replacement for a well-resourced class library. A well-stocked classroom library should have picture books, illustrated dictionaries, books about the student's home country, joke books, poetry, novels and nonfiction material. If possible, have books available that are written in the student's home language.

Explicitly teach word-learning strategies

Chapters 5, 6 and 7, although not specifically written for English-language learners, include examples of how to go about teaching word-learning strategies. These strategies apply to all English-language learners, native and non-native.

Word cards

Nation (2005, p. 590) claims there is substantial research to support the use of word cards: "such learning is very efficient and effective". Word cards should be used in conjunction with many opportunities to use the words in meaningful contexts. An advantage of using word cards is that they can be individualised. Students can also carry them in their pocket.

Words taken from word lists, reading material and content area reading are printed on one side and, if possible, the first-language translation is printed on the reverse side. Alternatively, a picture matching the word can be placed on the opposite side (e.g., picture of a book or chair or pilot or kiwi). Nation (2005) recommends the learner carry about 50 cards around with them and read through the cards whenever they are free. Students should be encouraged to identify the meaning of the word before turning the card over, and to say the word out loud.

Dictionary and thesaurus

Students should be encouraged to use a dictionary and thesaurus (Nation, 2005). Dictionary use can be problematic for learners (e.g., selecting the wrong definition). Dictionaries can, however, be used to confirm a guess or to clarify meaning.

Vocabulary-building Internet sites

There are a number of computer-based word-learning and vocabulary programs. Several sites that may be useful for primary-aged students include:
- http://www.manythings.org/lulu/ (English vocabulary games with pictures: word-to-picture and picture-to-word)
- http://eslbears.homestead.com/Contact_Info.html (vocabulary games: synonyms, opposites, animals, etc.)
- http://a4esl.org/a/v.html (this site, a project of *The Internet TESL Journal*, has over 1,000 activities for English-language learners).

Summary

There are at least three take-home messages in this chapter. First, it is a reality for the modern teacher that at least some of their pupils are likely to come from homes where English is a second language. Sometimes these pupils can decode well but need to read simpler material because their English vocabulary knowledge is not up to it. Sometimes they can neither decode nor understand the English words they read or listen to. In the United States it is estimated that nearly 25 percent of pupils in the school system are in this situation. In New Zealand, there are many classrooms with at least one English-language learner and many where there is more than one. These pupils may already know a lot of words in their own language, except they do not know how to express these meanings in English.

Second, a recommended strategy to learn words in English is to take advantage of the frequency principle in that a small proportion of words accounts for most of the words we read and hear. Learning this small number is a huge advantage for an English-language beginner. For example, the most frequent 100 words account for 50 percent of all the words we read and hear. The most frequent 1,000 words account for 70 to 80 percent of all the words we read and hear. Yes, the final 20 percent of words we read and hear stretches over a long list of more than 125,000 words, but learning the first 1,000 is obviously a good starting strategy.

Third, it is a good idea to assess the vocabulary knowledge of an English-language learner and we suggested a measure such as the *Peabody Picture Vocabulary Test*, which is given verbally, or the *Progressive Achievement Test* or the *STAR* Test, though the last two tests require the student to be able to read as well as understand. The teacher can then design vocabulary lessons and experiences according to the individual needs of each student. Fourth, the English-language learner can learn many English words by using context clues in reading (that is, by reading and listening to high-interest printed materials), and we suggested that the teacher make use of Ministry of Education *School Journals* and graded reading material to do this. There is actually a Ministry of Education website to help teachers locate appropriate material.

Fourth, we explained a number of teaching strategies that teachers can use to help the English-language learner to gain new vocabulary, including lots of exposure to oral language, discussion with other students and so on.

To conclude, we have suggested in this chapter that teachers need to be strategic when teaching English-language learners, so that they learn as much English vocabulary as possible, as quickly as possible. We have suggested that teachers target the high-frequency words of English, and give lots of reading experience and language experience at the right level of difficulty to get maximum growth in vocabulary learning. We agree with Helman (2009, p. 136) who recommends that when helping English-language learners, teachers "reach for the stars, but prioritise"—that is, to be strategic in your teaching so as to get the most gains in vocabulary learning. Teachers with high expectations who develop an instructional programme that caters for the needs of English-language learners, who are understanding and have empathy for their students, and who create a classroom environment that is conducive to English-language learners, will get great results!

PART 2: PRACTICE

Introduction

An anonymous joke

News release:

Two trucks loaded with thousands of copies of the *Oxford Dictionary and Thesaurus* crashed into each other as they were leaving a publishing house.

Witnesses were aghast, amazed, appalled, astonished, astounded, bemused, benumbed, bewildered, confounded, confused, dazed, dazzled, disconcerted, disoriented, dumbstruck, electrified, flabbergasted, horrified, immobilized, incredulous, nonplussed, overwhelmed, paralysed, perplexed, scared, shocked, startled, stunned, stupefied, surprised, taken aback, traumatized, upset.

As we have seen in Chapter 2, vocabulary knowledge is a critical component of reading comprehension and success in school. One writer has put it this way: "vocabulary knowledge *is* knowledge" (Stahl, 2005, p. 95). Other writers have commented on the importance of vocabulary not just for knowledge but as a tool of communication:

> A good vocabulary is the mark of an educated person—even when that person has not had the benefit of formal schooling. An individual with a skimpy vocabulary is at a handicap in conversation, oral and written expression, and listening and reading comprehension. (Johnson & Johnson, 1993, p. 212)

Graffiti writers might disagree with that quote. They seem quite happy to get their message across in just a few undecipherable words, but for the rest of us, having a good vocabulary helps us to get a lot more out of reading, writing, and even watching television. Also, understanding a joke, like this one from Woody Allen, requires a good vocabulary, like knowing the meaning of *immortality*: "I don't want to achieve immortality through my work ... I want to achieve it through not dying."

Vocabulary, knowing the meanings of lots of words, is extremely important and there are several ways to build a rich vocabulary. First, research shows that reading is a huge source of vocabulary (Stanovich, 2000). Second, teaching vocabulary to your students is an effective way of increasing their vocabulary. Third, vocabulary is enhanced when students are actively engaged and involved in using the vocabulary they have learnt. For example, it is one thing to know the meaning of *iconoclastic*, it is another to know how to use it.

Part 2 addresses the different ways in which teachers can assist their class to build vocabulary. First, since reading is important, we look at ways to encourage students to read. Second, given that teaching of vocabulary is supported by research, we look at ways to teach vocabulary. Third, since student involvement and engagement are necessary to build vocabulary, we look at ways to fit vocabulary instruction into the life of a busy classroom.

We recommend five ways to enhance vocabulary. The first is through reading—including the use of contextual clues. Why?—because authors give clues to the meanings of unusual words or explain them directly in the text. The second way is to teach word analysis techniques; how to break new words into meaningful parts, like breaking up compound words or, in the case of Latin words, breaking them into prefixes, root words and suffixes. The third way is to look at words in terms of their features. Even a simple word like *wall* can have many aspects to it, like different kinds of walls (walls of castles, Berlin Wall, Great Wall of China, garden walls, etc.); or to compare and contrast words, as in synonyms and antonyms; or to grade words (e.g., grades of emotions from depressed to exaltant). Concept maps provide a way of organising the different features of words. The fourth way is knowing about the multiple meanings of words. For example, even a simple word like *run* takes up about a page of the dictionary with at least 50 meanings. The fifth way is to use the dictionary and thesaurus, fabulous reseources that should not be gathering dust in the classroom.

These five strategies are all effective techniques, which we will explain in more detail in the next chapters where we take a closer look at each strategy. In Chapter 4 we discuss the role of reading; that is, print exposure in vocabulary acquisition, including contextual clues in text. Chapter 5 discusses how to go about teaching word analysis. Knowing about word parts and their meanings has a positive effect on vocabulary. Chapter 6 focuses on using concept maps to learn new words. Chapter 7 explores multiple meanings of words as well as figurative language. Students need to know that many "everyday" words have more than one meaning. Chapter 8 focuses on the dictionary and thesaurus, two important tools students can use to enhance their vocabulary.

CHAPTER 4

Increasing Vocabulary through Reading

This chapter looks at the way in which the simple act of reading can increase vocabulary. There is a weight of studies that recommend extensive reading as the best way to build vocabulary knowledge (Beck & McKeown, 1991; Nagy & Anderson, 1984; Nagy, Anderson, & Herman, 1987; Stahl & Stahl, 2004; Stanovich, 1986, 2000; Sternberg, 1987).

This incidental learning of words, through sheer volume of reading, may be the most significant factor in accounting for individual differences in vocabulary knowledge beyond the age of 10 (Stanovich, 1986, 2000). The best advice you can give a student to increase their vocabulary is to read. The problem is that most students (and adults) do not follow this advice. It's a bit like the advice that exercise is good for your health. Most of us agree, but still do not do it. The comedian Jimmy Durante was famous for saying, "One day I read a book; some day I'll read another." It's a joke that makes fun about reading, knowing that a lot of people, including many teachers, are not enthusiastic about reading (Nathanson, Pruslow, & Levitt, 2008).

It's not clear why many adults and students lack enthusiasm for reading. It may be that reading is seen as wasting time when they could be doing something more productive. Charles Dickens made fun of this attitude in the novel, *Bleak House*, where at one point in the story Mr Smallweed, who is a greedy, mean and spiteful character, is asked if he reads or gets read to, and he replies, "No, no. We have never been readers in this family. It don't pay. Stuff. Idleness. Folly. No, no!"

Whatever the reasons for not wanting to read, New Zealand research suggests that students are definitely becoming less enthusiastic about reading. In 2008, only 21 percent of Year 4s and 20 percent of Year 8s ranked reading as one of their top three leisure activities. This was a 10 percent drop from the same survey in 2000 (National Education Monitoring Project, 2009).

Can vocabulary increase without reading books? Obviously, yes. Just watching television or movies can sometimes have you reaching for the dictionary; for example, when the weather forecaster says that the next few days will be *salubrious* (that is, favourable), or when a character in a movie says that she feels *discombobulated* (that is, confused). In this chapter, though, we will focus on reading as a major way to improve vocabulary.

The benefits to vocabulary from reading books

Hayes and Ahrens (1988) analysed the type of words found in printed text, television texts and adult speech. They ranked the words used in the three contexts based on the frequency with which they occur. This analysis showed that students are 50 percent more likely to learn new words by reading than by listening to adults talking or by watching television.

They found that the number of rare words per 1,000 words in children's books is 30.9, as compared to 17.3 rare words per 1,000 for college graduates talking to friends, 22.7 rare words per 1,000 on prime-time adult television and 20.2 rare words per 1,000 on prime-time children's programmes. Children's books have 50 percent more rare words than the conversation of adults or prime-time television.

Reading makes you smarter

Reading has other benefits as well. These benefits include not just increased vocabulary, but fluency, general knowledge, verbal skills and comprehension. Stanovich (1993, p. 171) puts it like this:

> If 'smarter' means having a larger vocabulary and more world knowledge in addition to the abstract reasoning skills encompassed within the concept of intelligence, as it does in most laymen's definitions of intelligence, then reading may *well* make people smarter.

Cunningham and Stanovich (1998), write that:

> All of our studies have demonstrated that reading yields significant dividends for everyone—not just the 'smart kids' or the more able readers. Even the child with limited reading and comprehension skills will build vocabulary and cognitive structures through reading. (p. 14)

The value of rich context clues in text

Reading is a good way to learn new words because writers are often very considerate to their readers in terms of helping them to work out the meanings of words. When we come across a new word in a text, it is often in an appropriate context and there are often other clues in the text that are provided by the author to help the reader work out the meaning of the word. An example of helpful context is explained in Calfee and Patrick (1995), in that some writers give lots of information in the text to help work out unfamiliar words, as in *gullible* and *runt* in passages from the novel *Charlotte's Web* (White, 1952, p. 69):

> "I was just thinking, that people are very gullible," said Charlotte.
>
> "What does gullible mean?"
>
> "Easy to fool," said the spider.

"Well", said her mother, "one of the pigs is a runt. It is small and weak, and it will never amount to anything."

This piece of text offers very strong context clues that the reader can use to incorporate a new word like *gullible* and runt into their mental dictionary. The explanation for *gullible* is right there in the text, that it means "easy to fool". The explanation for runt is also right there. It means "small and weak and will never amount to anything."

White (1952, p. 113) uses a similar technique to define *versatile*:

"What does 'versatile' mean—full of eggs?" asked Wilbur.

"Certainly not," said Charlotte. "Versatile" means I can turn with ease from one thing to another. It means I don't have to limit my activities to spinning and trapping and stunts like that."

Sometimes the author's clues are implicit, so that inference is required. The following is an example of the author using implicit context clues to explain to the reader the word *inventing*. For example:

"Fern!", snapped her mother. "Stop it! Stop inventing these wild tales!" "I'm not inventing," said Fern. "I'm just telling you the facts" (White, 1952, p. 104).

Sometimes the context does not fully explain the meaning but it does give sufficient clues. For example, imagine you had to figure out the meaning of the made-up word *grubel* in the following passage:

Text: With her new compass, month's supply of food, and stubborn *grubel*, the old prospector rode out once more to find the lost gold mine. A *grubel* is: (a) an old fashioned backpack, (b) a new kind of 4-wheel drive, (c) a secret map made of oilcloth, (d) a horse or donkey.

The meaning of *grubel* seems to be a horse or a donkey. The context clues rule out other possibilities. In this way, the writer helps the reader by giving enough context to work out the meaning without actually defining the word.

The problem is that context is not always helpful. In a review of 21 studies on the use of context clues, it was found that context clues are effective, but only mildly so (Fukkink & de Glopper, 1998). Direct teaching of vocabulary is actually more effective than context clues (Hattie, 2009). Everyone would agree, though, that context clues are a lot more helpful than nothing at all, and that reading is a great way to take advantage of such clues.

The lesson learnt from the research is yes, try to get the meaning from context if you can, but be sure to have some back-up strategies as well, such as a dictionary or thesaurus you can turn to if the clues are confusing or non-existent.

Practical implications for teachers

The practical implications for teachers that we cover in the rest of this chapter are:

- Provide an inviting print-rich and technology-rich class library.
- Know what motivates readers, particularly reluctant readers, to read.
- Encourage and set goals for reading: ensure your students know that you believe in reading and that reading will take them somewhere.
- Read to and talk with your students.
- Teach how to use context to unlock the meaning of words.

Provide an inviting print-rich and technology-rich class library

The National Reading Research Center (1994) found that class and personal libraries are important influences in motivating 8–10-year-old children to read. The reality of many classroom libraries, however, is that they are cramped for space. In addition, resources may be inadequate. Figure 4.1 presents a useful checklist for setting up a class library. Stocking a classroom library when there are limited resources (e.g., restrictions on the number of books that can be issued from the school library, and sourcing books for a wide range of reader interest and ability) does present challenges for the classroom teacher. But these challenges can be overcome in a number of ways. For example:

- Ask parents to consider donating a book their child has read.
- Visit second-hand book stores.
- Attend garage and kerbside sales.
- Visit or write to local Rotary clubs.

In relation to this last point, literacy has been an international focus for Rotary since 1986 and there are over 250 Rotary Clubs in New Zealand. Each year the Rotary International President calls for Rotarians to support literacy projects. In March 2009 Rotary International President Dong Kurn Lee stated:

> As we celebrate Literacy Month this March, we are confronted by the monumental challenge of helping nearly a billion people experience the essential pleasure and power of reading and writing. Without these fundamental skills, too many of our friends and neighbors will remain trapped by poverty, hunger, and disease. (http://www.rotary.org/en/AboutUs/Rotaryleadership/RIpresident/Pages/ Literacy.aspx)

FIGURE 4.1: LIBRARY READING MATERIAL AND PHYSICAL SET-UP CHECKLIST

The following checklist may provide a useful guide when stocking your class library.

READING MATERIAL	YES	NO
Nonfiction		
Is there a variety of nonfiction books?		
Are the books engaging?		
Are the books comprehensible?		
Narrative		
Is there a variety of narrative books?		
Novels: (e.g., fantasy, scary, historical fiction adventure, humorous, etc.)		
Picture books		
Fairy tales		
Traditional tales		
Contemporary stories		
Poetry		
Joke books		
Magazines		
Comics		
Reference books (e.g., Guinness Book of Records)		
Books for NESB children (books written in their first language)		
PHYSICAL SET-UP		
Physically attractive		
Multiple copies of popular books		
Highly visible		
Accommodating several children		
Large pillows/comfy chair/s/two-seater couch		
CD player		
Computer		
Consider how your library will be organised A library with 200+ books (some suggest 5+ books per student) requires organisation. Will you divide into fiction/nonfiction/magazines? Arrange by author surname? Have a checkout system? Organise helpers to repair damaged books?		

The classroom library

Remember that the classroom library may be the main source of books for the students in your class. What's more, the books are not down the hall or in the school library that is visited 30 minutes once a week. Instead, books are within a few metres of the reader throughout the school day.

Before stocking your classroom library a suggestion is to carry out a survey of class interests. The survey below (Figure 4.2), designed for 12- and 13-year-olds, is from Worthy, Moorman and Turner (1999). It could easily be adapted for younger readers aged 8–11 years.

FIGURE 4.2: READING PREFERENCE SURVEY

PART 1: Reading preferences. Which of the following kinds of reading material would you be most interested in reading? Please listen as each item is read and discussed. Then put a tick by those materials that you would choose to read if they were available and you had time to read. If you have a comment or want to write a title, you may do so underneath each item. Raise your hand if you have questions.

1. _____ Young adult adventure novels
2. _____ Young adult funny novels
3. _____ Young adult novels about things that happen to people
4. _____ Young adult novels about science fiction or fantasy
5. _____ Scary books
6. _____ Biographies
7. _____ Series books
8. _____ Information books or magazines about sports
9. _____ Magazines about people
10. _____ Information books and magazines about cars and trucks
11. _____ Books that are mostly for adults.
    Write your favourite title(s) or author(s):
12. _____ Poetry books
13. _____ Encyclopaedias or books that give information about different things
14. _____ Almanacs or record books
15. _____ Drawing books
16. _____ Cartoons and comics
17. _____ Animals
18. _____ History or historical fiction
19. _____ Information books: science/math
20. _____ Picture books
21. _____ Other books or magazines
    Write your favourite title(s) or author(s):

PART 2: Reading habits and preferences. Please listen as the following questions are read and then answer them. Raise your hand if you have questions.

1. If you could read anything that you wanted to read, what would it be?
2. Who is your favourite author?
3. Where do you usually get your reading materials? Circle one.

school library	public library	store _____
		which one?
home	classroom	other _____
friends		

Source: Based on Worthy et al., 1999, p. 26

INCREASING VOCABULARY THROUGH READING

Students need time in class to read from the class library. This can be done by slotting a small amount of time, say 15 minutes, into the daily class schedule each day or every other day. It also means stocking the class library with interesting books. Imagine a class of 12-13 year olds totally engaged in the reading of "good" books like *Goodnight Mr Tom*, *The Silver Sword*, or *The Cay*. These three novels have appeared on a number of "good books to read" lists prepared by library associations or stores such as Whitcoulls and Borders. After 15 minutes of silent reading the teacher informs the class that it is time to do maths, or writing, or science or social studies. The class continues reading largely ignoring the teacher's request to stop. The teacher raises her voice ever so slightly and repeats the announcement. Students reluctantly stop reading and prepare for the next subject. What a great vindication for having a class library to have students so absorbed in reading.

There are many advantages in reading books of fiction and nonfiction in that students are exposed to sustained pieces of writing but it can be argued that the class library should include material other than books. Hayes and Ahrens (1988) found that popular magazines, comics and newspapers had more rare words than children's books. Popular magazines had 65.7 rare words per 1,000 written, comic books had 53.5 rare words per 1,000 and newspapers had 68.3 per 1,000—compared to 30.9 for children's books. Restricting students' reading diet may impact negatively on their attitude towards reading. A suggestion that would provide students with the chance to read books and nonbooks would be to assign one or two days each week where students can read popular magazines, comics and newspapers.

When sourcing books for your class library the following websites may be helpful:

International Reading Association & Children's Book Council:
Children's Choices list:
http://www.cbcbooks.org/readinglists/childrenschoices

Caldecott Medal winners:
http://www.ala.org/ala/mgrps/divs/alsc/awardsgrants/bookmedia/caldecottmedal/caldecottmedal.cfm

Newberry Medal winners:
http://www.ala.org/ala/mgrps/divs/alsc/awardsgrants/bookmedia/newberymedal/newberyhonors/newberymedal.cfm

Fractor, Woodruff, Martinez and Teale (1993) list a number of criteria for assessing the quality of classroom libraries. They recommend:

- at least 1 book per pupil (basic)—5 is good, and 8 is excellent
- enough space to accommodate 3 children (basic)—4 is good, 5 is excellent

- seating or carpeting, a quiet area, good lighting
- a partition from rest of room, open faced presentation of books, books organised so that pupils know what books are for their group (this would help students to choose a book that is not too hard)
- attractive book jackets.

Electronic texts

Children can also access electronic texts. The following sites may be suitable for your classroom.

Children's Storybooks Online. This website has books for young children, older children and young adults. Click on the age-group (e.g., young children) then click titles that have 🔊 . These titles have audio included with the story. Book titles without the icon (🔊) include text and pictures only. http://www.magickeys.com/books/

Morris Gleitzman: Australian children's author Morris Gleitzman also has an excellent website. Children are able to listen in read-along style to unabridged recordings of chapters from every one of Gleitzman's books, including his most recent book, *Toad Surprise*. Most of Morris Gleitzman's books are also available on audio-books: http://www.morrisgleitzman.com/

Reading Rockets. This site includes interviews with well-known authors and illustrators. Authors include Judy Blume, Lois Lowry, Mem Fox and Jon Scieszka. Children will enjoy hearing authors and illustrators talk about their work. http://www.readingrockets.org/books/interview

Know what motivates readers, particularly reluctant readers, to read

The National Reading Research Center (1994) found that children aged 8–10 years place a high priority on reading books they hear about from others, including friends, parents and teachers. Children's comments included:

> "… my friend Kristin was reading it and told me about it and I said, Hmmmmm, that sounds pretty interesting."

> "I'm in the lower reading group … I heard the other group reading it, so I checked it out in the library."

> "I heard about them from my teachers … they read good books to us."

> "I read it after the teacher read it aloud".

> "I'm rereading that book."

> "I want to read *Stuart Little* … my mom read it to us". (p. 177)

INCREASING VOCABULARY THROUGH READING

Having access to books through well-stocked and appropriate reading material in classroom libraries, or by regular visits to school and local libraries, has an impact on motivation to read. Joining the local library (like joining a club) and being issued with a library card can be highly motivating for some pupils.

Good book solution

Some readers enjoy browsing through the library, but others find it daunting. What they see is a "sea of spines" and they do not know which books are the "good ones" to read. What's more, reading is not a favourite activity, so class trips to the school library can mean wandering around chatting to friends, or heading straight for the comfy chairs or couch. Reading is not on some students' agenda.

One teacher came up with a subtle, yet effective, way of motivating her students to read (Beers, 1996). The teacher, before her weekly library visit, asked the school librarian to select 30 suitable books for her "aliterate" readers (those who can read but choose not to). The librarian put the 30 books into a box attractively labelled "Good Books". The box was then placed near the librarian's desk. When the class arrived the librarian carried on with her work—not wanting to bring the students' attention to the box of books. Instead, she wanted the students to discover the books themselves.

In time, the box was noticed by one of the aliterate students. The student began browsing through the box, having asked the librarian, "Are these the good books?" The librarian nodded, and continued with her work. Before long other students began browsing the box of "Good Books". They each checked out a book.

They didn't know authors, didn't know genre and didn't know where to look for the proverbial "good book". Narrowing the choice allowed them to "shop" in a smaller place and still feel independent in their selection.

The following week the students returned to the library and there was another box of books labelled "More Good Books". Students continued to borrow books from the two boxes. A number of weeks later one of the students told the librarian that the book he had selected the previous week was "not good". What was the librarian's response? She put a third box on the desk with the label, "Not Good". Before long, two students were sharing their views on why the book was good and why it wasn't.

Soon these two students, who six weeks earlier never checked out or read any books, were discussing what made this book good and bad. A third student snatched the book and declared, "I'll read it and tell y'all next week if it's good or not" (Beers, 1996, p. 113).

See the movie first

Encourage students to see movies that have been made into books. Students can see the movie *Holes* (Sachar, 1998) before reading the book, or the movie *Harry Potter and the Philosopher's Stone* (Rowling, 1997) before reading the book.

A Google search using the key words "children's books and movies" will result in a number of sites that list children's books that have been made into feature films. Wikipedia is one site. Although the list is not complete (Wikipedia acknowledges this), it provides teachers with a list of movies that may be suitable for some of their students. Table 4.1 gives a small sample of children's books that have been made into movies.

TABLE 4.1: SOME CHILDREN'S BOOKS THAT HAVE BEEN MADE INTO MOVIES

BOOK TITLE and AUTHOR	NAME OF MOVIE	MOVIE RELEASED
Stormbreaker (Anthony Horowitz)	*Alex Rider: Operation Stormbreaker*	2007
The BFG (Roald Dahl)	*The BFG*	1989
Bridge to Terabithia (Katherine Paterson)	*Bridge to Terabithia*	2007
The Cat in the Hat (Dr Seuss)	*The Cat in the Hat*	2003
Charlie and the Chocolate Factory (Roald Dahl)	*Willy Wonka and the Chocolate Factory* *Charlie and the Chocolate Factory*	1971 2005
Charlotte's Web (E.B. White)	*Charlotte's Web*	2006
Curious George (H.A. Rey & M. Rey)	*Curious George*	2006
Freaky Friday (Mary Rodgers)	*Freaky Friday*	2003
Harry Potter series (J.K. Rowling)	Harry Potter series	2001, 2002, 2004, 2005, 2007
How to Eat Fried Worms (Thomas Rockwell)	*How to Eat Fried Worms*	2006
The Lion, the Witch and the Wardrobe (C.S. Lewis)	*The Lion, the Witch and the Wardrobe*	2005
Nim's Island (Wendy Orr and Kerry Millard)	*Nim's Island*	2008
Tales of Despereaux (Kate Dicamillo)	*Tales of Despereaux*	2008
Fantastic Mr Fox (Roald Dahl)	*Fantastic Mr Fox*	2010
Alice in Wonderland (Lewis Carroll)	*Alice in Wonderland*	2010

INCREASING VOCABULARY THROUGH READING

Encourage and set goals for reading

Ensure your students know that you believe in reading and that reading will take them somewhere. Consider the success of the fast-food chains McDonalds and KFC, or any product that has sold well. Sales success can, in part, be attributed to marketing. Teachers must also market their product—the product of reading. How can teachers market reading?

Book sell

For reluctant and aliterate readers, selecting a "good" book to read presents challenges. Some children find it difficult to select books to read. They don't know where to start. Book sell (or book sharing time) is one way of marketing reading. According to Ward (1997, p. 22):

> Book sell is one way of enthusing readers about books. It is a time when the teacher and children explain about books they've read from the class library and pass them on for others to read.

Reading log

Encourage your students to keep a reading log. Make an A4 sheet as in the sample reading log below (Figure 4.3) and have pupils stick it into the front of their class reading or writing books. This enables teachers to provide feedback on what students are reading, offer suggestions for further reading, and monitor the volume and type of reading children are doing. The reading log can become a point of discussion: "Jack, tell me why you liked this book." "Why didn't you like this book?" "Why did you read a few pages and put the book back?" Let children know that you also put books back: that it is OK to read a few pages, decide it is not a book you want to read and then return it.

Here is a sample reading log.

FIGURE 4.3: SAMPLE READING LOG

DATE	TITLE	NO. OF PAGES READ	RATING (ONCE FINISHED)	SIGNATURE
			😃 😊 😐 ☹	
			😃 😊 😐 ☹	
			😃 😊 😐 ☹	
			😃 😊 😐 ☹	

Literacy quiz

Hold a class book quiz. This could lead on to the local (and national) Kids' Lit Quiz organised by Wayne Mills at The University of Auckland. Although The Kids' Lit Quiz is for Years 7 and 8 students, Years 1–6 classroom teachers and syndicates could organise their own, less formal book quiz. Quizzes could be themed (e.g., Roald Dahl or Margaret Mahy books; picture books; books that have been made into films; or individual books, including one the teacher has read). If children work in teams then no child is singled out for their in-depth knowledge of books or their lack of knowledge. Instead, the quiz is the result of team work. The literacy quiz should be a fun class or syndicate activity.

Set goals for, and model, reading

In a study of Years 5/6 and 7/8 exemplary reading teachers, Dymock (2008) found that exemplary teachers encourage and set goals for lots of reading. Years 1–4 teachers should begin by providing five minutes a day for independent reading and slowly increase the time over the term to 10 minutes. Years 5–8 teachers should begin with 10 minutes and slowly increase the time allocated for independent reading to approximately 20 minutes. Reading times will vary from class to class.

Dymock (2008) also found that exemplary teachers model reading. As one teacher put it, "If I expect them to do reading, you know, I'm not busy trying to figure out what I'm doing the rest of the day. I actually put myself next to a kid and I read and I read and I turn the pages" (Believe in Reading, slide 35). Nathanson et al. (2008, p. 313) asked the question: "Do children learn because of what we, as teachers, say, or do they learn by observing what teachers do and how teachers behave?" We believe that "children see—children do". Children who see their teacher read, and listen to their teacher talk about books they have read, will be more motivated to read than students in a class where the teacher is setting up the science lesson, marking books or chatting to a colleague while the class is silent reading.

After-school reading should also be encouraged. Again, the initial goal should be for five–ten minutes each day, and increased over a period of time.

As we have seen, to increase their vocabulary, children should be reading age-appropriate texts. Steer them toward books that have challenging vocabulary but be sure that they can decode the books. Children experiencing decoding difficulties who absolutely refuse to read can listen to books, *School Journal* stories and articles that can be read to them by you the teacher or by their parents or by older pupils at the school, or that have been recorded on CD, or book extracts that are read and available online.

INCREASING VOCABULARY THROUGH READING

One teacher in Dymock's (2008) study used an example to explain the importance of building reading mileage. She reported the following conversation in class:

> My brother went for his pilot licence. He wanted to be a pilot so he had to build up time. He had to do so many hours up in the sky. In order for you to become good readers you're going to have to build up some mileage.
>
> "How do we build up mileage Miss?" asked one kid.
>
> "We actually have to read."
>
> "Is that all?"

Read to and talk with your students

Reading aloud to children is a feature of Years 0–4 classrooms. One reason for this is that Years 0–4 children are learning to read. That is, they are, still developing their decoding skills. New Zealand researchers have also found that pupils do learn new words when listening to stories, and this is especially so if the teacher discusses or explains the new words with them, either during or after reading (Elley, 1989; Nicholson & Whyte, 1992).

Teale (2003, p. 123), raises a number of questions every teacher should consider:

- How much should I read aloud? Although Teale did not give a definite number, a suggestion is about 15 minutes a day for six–eight-year-olds. and 20 minutes a day for older children.
- What should I read? A good source of books to read is *The Read-Aloud Handbook* (Trelease, 2006). Consider the book quality, type of book and the children's backgrounds, age and interests. Also consider the purpose of the reading (e.g., enjoyment, instructional).
- How should I read to children? Consider eye contact, management, voice/inflection and the flow of the story. Also ensure children can see you. If the book has pictures, make sure the children can see the pictures.
- How does what I read aloud fit into the *The New Zealand Curriculum*? Consider how a book fits into the unit being studied, connections among the books that are being read aloud, and opportunities for responses to or extensions of the book beyond the actual reading.

Mem Fox (*Reading Magic*, 2001, pp. 35-47) gives some suggestions for reading stories aloud to your class:

1. Consider the children's background, age, and interests when selecting a book to read.
2. Make sure the children can see you. If reading a picture book check to see if the children can see the pictures.

3. Are the children comfortable?

4. Be familiar with the story. Maintain your enthusiasm even if you have read it many times before.

5. The first line of the story has to be sensational! Try practising that first line at home—how can you make 'Once upon a time' sound so good that it will grab your audience? You will know immediately if you have grabbed them. If they are sitting on the mat in front of you, they will start creeping forward to hear you better.

6. Be as expressive as possible, vary your voice, emphasise some words, e.g., "there once was a *baby* kitten".

7. The eyes and voice are important, make sure there is eye contact, the eyes widen, narrow, etc., that your face is animated, that is is happy, sad, keen, surprised, etc., that your body language is a little bit OTT, that is, enthusiastic, move your head, jump with surprise, etc.

8. Make sure the voice is interesting, not cutesy, or saccharine, or condescending. Make your voice do gymnastics: loud, soft, fast, slow, high, low, e.g., slow voice for sad or scary parts, fast voice for fast parts, low voice for scary parts, long pause for suspense parts. It is often good to read quickly—children have no problem with that. Too slow can be boring.

9. The last line has to be terrific, satisfying, and complete. If you read it too fast, you can ruin the feeling. Read it slowly, drag it out. "And—they—lived …."

Remember that your enthusiasm is infectious. We recommend you select a regular time to read aloud to your class. Read nonfiction, narratives (e.g., picture books, short stories, novels) and poetry, as well as newspaper and magazine articles. In addition to reading to your class for sheer pleasure, remember to talk with your class (or small groups) about the material being read. Research suggests that children's vocabulary increases more when the teacher reads to the class and talks with them about the story and any interesting words in it, before, during and after reading.

The secret of how vocabulary increases by reading and listening to text is well explained by Stanovich (2000, p. 254):

> … —how children's vocabularies grow at prodigious rates despite the seeming inefficacy of direct instruction in vocabulary—can be explained by the effects of mere exposure. Specifically, when a new word is encountered in the context of other known words, it is not just the representation of the unknown word that is sharpened, but that of all other words in the lexicon.

Teach how to use context clues to unlock the meaning of words

Using context relies on knowing the surrounding words and context also relies on having some understanding of the strategies that are discussed in the following chapters. For example, to infer the meaning of *telemeter* (in the story it was used for measuring the beat of the heart for a character in the story who had heart problems) using context clues from the following sentences would be challenging for young readers: "He had to have a box with some wires on it on his chest. Mum explained that the box was called a telemeter"(McCallum, 2001, p. 23). If students had an understanding of word analysis (see Chapter 5 for more on word analysis) where they knew that *telemeter* comprised two Greek combining forms (*tele* + *meter*) and they knew the meaning of each word part (*tele*—distance; *meter*—measure) they would combine the use of context clues and word analysis to infer the meaning. Students should also be encouraged to verify their thinking about the meaning by checking a dictionary or thesaurus.

Goerss, Beck and McKeown (1999) suggest additional strategies for making use of context clues. In relation to the above passage, this might involve:

1. Read and then reread. The passage is reread in order to highlight the unfamiliar word.

2. Discuss context. It is important to discern whether students have an overall understanding of the text. [Note: If most of the words are unknown to the student, context will not be helpful.]

3. Initial hypothesis. Students make an initial hypothesis and provide a reason for their hypothesis.

4. Guide the student. The teacher helps guide the student—questioning or probing to gain additional information from context. and explaining to students that context may not provide enough clues to determine the meaning of the word, that other strategies might be needed such as word analysis and use of the dictionary.

5. Summary. Together with the students summarise what context can and cannot tell you about the word.

The Exciting Books List

This list is supplied by Joan Gibbons from the Wintec Library, Hamilton

Books for ages 4–14 (* = Highly recommended)

Picture books

Bishop, Gavin. (2007). *Rats!* Auckland: Random House. (4–8)

Briggs, Raymond. (1973). *Jim and the beanstalk*. London: Puffin. (4–8)

Burton, Virginia Lee. (1941). *Calico the wonder horse*. New York: Houghton Mifflin. (4–8)

Crew, Gary & Woolman, S. (1997). *Watertower*. Flinders Park, SA: Era. And others. (7–12)*

Gravett, Emily. (2005). *Wolves*. London: Macmillan. (4–10)

Leaf, Munro. (1937). *The story of Ferdinand*. London: Hamish Hamilton. (3–7)

Macaulay, David. (1990). *Black and white*.* Boston: Houghton Mifflin. (5–12)

Macaulay, David. (1995). *Shortcut*. Boston: Houghton Mifflin. (5–12)

Mahy, Margaret & Allen, J. (1989). *The great white man-eating shark*. London: Puffin. (4–8)

McNaughton, Colin. (2002). *Boo!* London: Collins; *Who's that dancing on the ceiling?* (4–7)

Oakley, Graham. (1972). *The church mouse*. London: Macmillan (series). (4–9)

Peet, Bill. (1977). *Big bad Bruce*. Boston: Houghton Mifflin. (4–8)

Ryan, John. (2001; first published 1957). *Captain Pugwash: A pirate story*. London: Red Fox (series). (4–8)

Scieszka, Jon & Smith, Lane. (2002; first published 1992). *The sticky cheeseman and other stories*. London: Puffin. (6–12)

Sendak, Maurice. (1963). *Where the wild things are*. New York: Harper & Row.

Sendak, Maurice. (1963). *In the night kitchen*. (2–7)

Thompson, Colin. (2006). *The short and incredibly happy life of Riley*. South Melbourne: Lothian. (4–9)

Van Allsburg, Chris. (1981). *Jumanji*. Boston: Houghton Mifflin. (6–12)

Weisner, David. (1991). *Tuesday*. New York: Clarion. (5–8)

Novels

Alexander, Lloyd. (2004; first published 1973). *The book of three*. London: Usborne. (Taran series) (9–13)

Beale, Fleur. (1993). *Slide the corner*. Auckland: Scholastic *Driving a bargain*. (10–14)

Breslin, Theresa. (1994). *Whispers in the graveyard*. London: Methuen. (10–13)

Catran, Ken. (2003). *Jacko Moran: Sniper*. South Melbourne: Lothian (series). (10–14)

Colfer, Eian. (2002). *Artemis Fowl*. London: Puffin (series). * (9–14)

Crossley-Holland, Kevin. (1985). *Storm*. London: Heinemann. (7–10)

Dahl, Roald. (1983). *The witches*. London: Cape. (7–12)*

DiTerlizzi, Tony & Black, Holly. (2003). *Spiderwick chronicles* (series). London: Simon & Schuster. (7–11)

Fine, Anne. (1994. *Flour babies*. London: Hamish Hamilton. (9–13)

Fleischmann, Sid. (1992; first published 1972). *McBroom's wonderful one-acre farm: Three tall tales*. New York: Greenwillow. (8–12)

Ford, Vince. (1999). *2MUCH4U*. Auckland: Scholastic. (9–13)

Gee, Maurice. (2006; first published 1979). *Under the mountain*. Auckland: Puffin. (9–13)

Gleitzman, Maurice. (1999). *Toad rage*. Ringwood, Vic.: Puffin. (9–13)

Hiasson, Carl. (2005). *Flush*. New York: Alfred J. Knopf. (9–13)

Horowitz, Anthony. (2001). *Stormbreaker*. London: Walker (series). (9–14)

Jennings, Paul. (1999). *Unreal!* Ringwood, Vic.: Penguin. (8–12)

Jones, Diana Wynne. (2003). *Charmed life*. London: Collins (Chrestomanci series 8–13); *Dark Lord of Derkholm* (1998), series 9–14. London: Gollancz.

Lewis, C. S. (1950). *The lion, the witch and the wardrobe*. London: Collins. (Narnia series, 8–12).

Mahy, Margaret. (1984). *The changeover* (12–15);

Mahy, Margaret. (2009) *The dark blue 100-ride bus ticket.* (7–12)
Morpurgo, Michael. (2003). *Private peaceful.* London: Collins. (9–13)
O'Brien, Robert. (1972). *Mrs Fisby and the rats of NIHM.* London: Gollancz. (8–12)
Orwin, Joanna. (2001). *Owl.* Dunedin: Longacre. (10–14)
Paterson, Katherine. (1978). *Bridge to Terabithia.* London: Gollancz.
Paulson, Gary. (1987). *Hatchet.* New York: Penguin. (9–14)*
Peck, Robert. (1998). *A long way from Chicago.* New York: Dial. (9–13)
Pilkey, Dav. (1998-). *Captain underpants* (series). New York: Scholastic. (7–12)
Pratchett, Terry. (1996). *Johnny and the bomb.* London: Doubleday.
Ridley, Philip. (2002; first published 1992). *Krindlekrax.* London: Faber. (9–12)
Rodda, Emily. (1994). *Rowan of Rin.* London: Scholastic (series); *Deltora quest* (series). (8–13)
Rowling, J. K. (1997). *Harry Potter and the philosopher's stone.* London: Bloomsbury (series). (8–14)
Sachar, Louis. (1998). *Holes.* New York: Dell. (9–14)*
Starke, Ruth. (2000). *Nips XI.* South Melbourne, Vic.: Lothian. (9–13)
Taylor, William. (1992). *Knitwits.* Auckland: Ashton Scholastic (series); *Agnes the sheep.* (9–13)
Tolkien, J. R. R. (1937). *The Hobbit; Lord of the rings* (series). (9–14)
Westall, Robert. (1982). *The machine gunners.* Harmondsworth: Puffin. (9–14)
Wilson, Jacqueline. (1995). *Double act.* London: Doubleday. (8–12); *Bad girls* (11–14)

Books for older teenagers (age 15–17)

Beale, Fleur. (1993). *Slide the corner.* Auckland: Scholastic.
Ford, Vince. (2006). *Boyz 'n bikes.* Auckland: Scholastic.
Horowitz, Anthony. (2009). *Crocodile tears.* London: Walker.
Mahy, Margaret. (1987). *Memory.* London: Dent.
Peck, Robert Newton. (1972). *The day no pigs would die.* New York: Knopf.
Peck, Robert. (2009). *Horse thief.* New York: Harper Collins.
Swindells, Robert. (1993). *Stone cold.* London: H. Hamilton.

Summary

In this chapter we have discussed the impact of reading on vocabulary. Research indicates that many students lack enthusiasm for reading. This chapter suggests five ways teachers can encourage their students to read: provide an inviting print-rich and technology-rich class library; know what motivates your students to read; encourage and set goals for reading; read to, and talk with, your students; and teach your students how to use context to unlock the meaning of words.

CHAPTER 5

Structural Analysis

Introduction

This chapter will discuss how to go about teaching vocabulary by breaking words into parts. Instruction will tackle the structures of Anglo-Saxon compound words, Latin words (with their prefixes and suffixes) and Greek combining forms. They are all part of the layers of the English language we discussed in Chapter 1. To become expert readers we need to know how words from these different languages are constructed, and how to deconstruct them to get to their meanings.

Structural analysis

Constructing and deconstructing meanings is called *structural analysis*. Structural analysis helps the pupil to deconstruct a long word into its parts and use the parts to construct the meaning. It is like phonics, except that instead of breaking the word into its sounds, you are breaking the word into familiar, meaningful parts (morphemes). It works best for words where the total word is not understood but it has familiar meaningful parts, so the student can reconstruct the meaning.

The process of breaking words into their meaningful parts is so important that some reading specialists argue that it is the first thing we should do when decoding the meaning of a word. It enables us to avoid mistakes, such as treating *sh* as a digraph that says /sh/ in words that have two meaningful parts, such as *mishap*. If we look for the meaningful parts of a word first, it makes it much easier to decode the word, and in turn get the right meaning. Certain word parts also have very predictable meanings, such as the *-s* ending that means plurality and the *-ed* ending that means the past tense.

Many young students do not know that words have these little meaningful parts, like *-s* and *-ed*, that help to work out their meaning. Pupils who do have this ability to analyse words in terms of their meaningful parts are good readers. It is part of what makes them good at reading. A litmus test of who knows about meaningful parts of words and who does not is to ask pupils to spell words like *trees* and *kissed*. The pupil who misspells *trees* as *treez*, or *kissed* as *kisst*, does not understand the nature of morphemes. Lack of such knowledge is not just a drawback in spelling, but in school achievement as well (Bryant & Nunes, 2004; Nunes & Bryant, 2006, 2009).

Recent research (Rosenthal & Ehri, 2008) indicates that we tend to overlook the importance of orthography, or spelling, in the learning of vocabulary, and vice versa; that is, learning the meanings of new words can

STRUCTURAL ANALYSIS

also influence our ability to decode and spell words. This is because linking spelling, meaning and decoding together has a powerful mnemonic value. *Mnemonic* is a Greek word for the mind, and means the art of remembering.

Everyone interested in improving their memory knows that it is easier to remember a word if they can associate it with something, like a word that sounds the same, or an image. For example, remembering the word *lachrymose*, which means tearful, is much easier if you associate it with an image of a sad person in a laundromat stuck with a huge pile of washing and crying; or with an image that sounds like the word, such as a lacquered moose (Levin, 1996)!

Connectionist theory argues that how we store words in our minds—with sound, spelling and meaning—helps to make it easier to remember words. The sounds of words in our mental dictionary (phonemes), their spellings and their meanings are all interconnected, and all act like glue to stick meanings in our memory (Ehri, 2005a, 2005b).

This is really important for teaching, because it means spelling is a very significant way of gluing words into memory and increasing our vocabulary (Ehri & Rosenthal, 2007). In one recent study (Rosenthal & Ehri, 2008; Rosenthal, 2009), teachers who explained the meanings of words, showed their students the spellings of the words, told them how to pronounce the words, helped them to sound out the words and showed them illustrations of the words produced better word learning than teachers who only talked about and showed pictures of the words. They found that showing the spellings of words and how to pronounce them acted as a glue to make a significant improvement in children's vocabulary. This helps to explain the puzzle as to why good readers seem to learn so many new words: they do a lot of reading, and they are good at breaking the spellings of words into meaningful parts, and this helps to cement the word meanings into memory.

How do you break a word into its meaningful parts?

Morphemes

A large proportion of words in English, and even more in other languages, have more than one morpheme. Linguists refer to structural analysis as morphemic analysis. The ability to break up morphemes when you decode the meaning of multi-morpheme words is important, especially for Latin-based words (see Chapter 1). The Romance languages, such as French, Italian and Spanish, have many Latin-based words. Latin uses affixation (i.e., prefixes and suffixes) to form words. The affixes are attached before (prefixes) the root word and after it (suffixes).

A definition of *morpheme* is that it is the smallest unit of meaning in a word or words. Deconstructing a word into its morphemes is quite easy if you think of the word as a combination of parts that you can take off and then replace with other parts. For example, the word *attached* can be broken into *a-ttach-ed*. We know *a-* is a morpheme because we can replace it with *de-* to make a new word, *detached*. Then we can also take off the *-ed*, and replace it with *-ing*, which has a sense of continuing to form *detaching*. And so on.

If you are still not sure what morphemes are, here are some words for you to consider. Read the list of words below (cover the second column before you start reading) and guess the number of morphemes in each word (see Moats, 2000).

TABLE 5.1: COUNTING MORPHEMES

WORD	NUMBER OF MORPHEMES	EXPLANATION
bookworm	2	Book and worm.
unicorn	2	Uni means one, and corn means horn.
elephant	1	It is one word, originates from Greek.
believed	2	Comes from Middle English, beleven plus addition of past tense morpheme -ed.
incredible	3	The base of the word is cred, from Latin, to believe, the -ible indicates it is an adjective, and the prefix in- means not; that is, not able to be believed.
finger	1	Finger is one word, meaning part of the hand, excluding the thumb, from Old English.
pies	2	The meaning of pie in this example is meat or fruit baked in pastry. Origin of word not known. The suffix -s means plural, more than one pie.
telegram	2	Tele means distance and gram means letter. The two morphemes originate from Greek. The word means to send a letter by telegraph which is an electronic way to send a message. Nowadays we would call it "email".
gardener	2	Garden is from the French jardin. The suffix -er means someone who does something. A gardener is someone who gardens.
attached	3	Attach has the meaning of fasten to something and is from the French attacher. The a- prefix means "onto". You can replace the a- with de- to form a new meaning, detached. The -ed suffix means past tense.
transportation	3	A Latin word. The prefix trans- means across, the root word port means carry and the suffix -ion means it is a noun.
windowsill	2	A compound word made of window and sill, meaning the lowest part of the window.

STRUCTURAL ANALYSIS

A morpheme can be very short or very long. A long morpheme is a word like *octopus*, *rhinoceros* or *salamander*. A short morpheme is the plural suffix *-s*. A two-morpheme word can have one long and one short morpheme; for example, *chickens* has two morphemes, *chicken* and *-s*.

Morphemes can be free or bound. Free morphemes stand alone as words in themselves; for example, *cat*, *table*. Compound words are made up of free morphemes; for example, *sunshine* (*sun* + *shine*). Bound morphemes have meaning only when they are part of other words; for example, prefixes like *ex-*, *re-*, *un-* and *-inter*; suffixes like *-s* and *-er*; and root words like *rupt* and *dict*. The bound root *rupt* (meaning *break*) has no meaning in itself, but it does get meaning when you add the prefix *inter-* to form *interrupt*. The tense can also be changed by adding the suffix *-ing*, to form *interrupting*. The meaning then becomes "breaking between", as in *interrupting* a conversation.

Two examples

Johnson and Pearson (1984) give the example of *unimaginable*. At first the pupil might have no idea what this means, but if they can recognise the known word *imagine* in the middle of the word, and if they recognise the two familiar parts, *un-* and *-able*, the meaning of the word will become clear. The meaning will be even clearer if the word is in a context like, "When Neil Armstrong was a child it would have been unimaginable to him that one day he would walk on the moon" (p. 127).

Durkin (1983) gives the example of the word *unenviable* in the context of the following sentence: "She was in the unenviable position of having to go back in the icy water again." A student who was thinking analytically about the word and trying to deconstruct it into morphemes might be thinking aloud the following: "The middle of the word is *envy*. The front of the word is *un-*. The back of the word is *-able*. So putting it together the word is *un-envy-able*. Right so what does it mean? The core of the word is *envy*, which means you wish you had something. But *un-* means you don't wish you had it which makes sense. I wouldn't want to have to climb back into that icy water again."

Demonstration lesson

An example of how to teach a guided reading lesson that focuses on vocabulary is given in the follow-up activities in this chapter. It shows how to select just a few words from the story that are suitable for structural analysis. It also shows how to combine the structural analysis of some words with a concept map for other words.

Analysing words from different origins

Anglo-Saxon words

The value of structural analysis is that it gives the pupil strategies that can be used to work out the meaning of a word that as a whole looks too hard, but if broken into familiar meaningful parts can have its meaning worked out. English has a lot of *compound* words, many of these from Anglo-Saxon (see Chapter 1), that are made up of two base words. Compound words can seem unfamiliar to a pupil. One of our pupils was able to read the word *rain* on its own, and *coat* on its own, but when shown *raincoat* said, "That's a long word—I can't read that", even though she knew how to read each base word on its own.

This is why we need to show pupils how to look for the familiar parts of a long word and in this way construct the meaning from the parts. Sometimes both base words in the compound word describe the meaning of the word, as in *overcoat* (a coat to put over you), *gumboot* (a boot made of gum—that is, rubber) and *raincoat* (a coat for the rain). Sometimes at least one of the morphemes is relevant; for example, *berry* in *strawberry* (which is a kind of berry). The compound word can sometimes be metaphorical, such as *bookworm* (someone who reads a lot of books). Lastly, some compound words are only vaguely suggestive, though they do have a little bit of meaning; for example, a *butterfly* is like a *fly* in the sense that it has wings and can fly but it is not like *butter*. Neither is a *ladybird* a *bird* like a *lady*. Some words are not compounds because the two parts do not relate to the meaning of the word and they are pronounced differently anyway, like *father* (which is not a compound of *fat* and *her*) and *some* (which is not a compound of *so* and *me*).

When grouping compound words for instruction, Johnson and Pearson (1984) suggest teaching them in categories so that pupils can more easily see the relationship between the two words. For example, if we label the two morphemes in a word A and B, in that order, in the word *riverbank*, the bank (B) is part of the river (A). This compound pattern is B of A. Here are some other examples:

- B of A: *weekend*, end of the week
- B is from A: *sunlight*, light from the sun
- B is for A: *paintbrush*, brush for painting
- B is like A: *pigtail*, tail like a pig's tail; *frogman*, man like a frog
- B is A: *blackbird*, bird is black; *strongman*, man is strong
- B does A: *towtruck*, truck does towing
- B with A: *wheelchair*, chair with wheels.

STRUCTURAL ANALYSIS

Anglo-Saxon words can also be *affixed* with prefixes and suffixes. The prefix is usually a preposition, like *over-* (overtake, overlook), *under-* (underbelly, underground), *in-* (inside, inroad) and so on. They also use suffixes, like *-ing* (walking, feeding), *-er* (robber, teacher), *-ly* (sadly, badly), *-ness* (kindness, goodness), *-ed* (jumped, wanted) and *-s* (cats, dogs). Anglo-Saxon suffixes can be inflections; that is, plural endings (cat/cat*s*), verb tense (walk/walk*ed*), possession (Tom/Tom*'s*) and comparison (happy/happi*er*). The suffixes can also change the derivation of the word (i.e., its part of speech) from a verb to an adjective, and so on (e.g., hope/hope*ful*).

Students can add many new Anglo-Saxon words to their mental dictionary through structural analysis, keeping in mind that each base word can turn into lots of other related words. For example, *run, runs, running* and *runner*. This is about as complicated as Anglo-Saxon words get. If you can read Anglo-Saxon words, then it is possible to reach an eight-year-old reading level.

Latin words

Structural analysis is a handy skill when it comes to long words. An eight-year-old pupil might be able to read *expect* but struggle with *unexpectedly*. The root word, *expect*, is from Latin, meaning "to look out for" (*spect* is in words like *spectacles*, for looking). The prefix *un-* means *not*. By using structural analysis, the pupil can break the word into familiar, meaningful parts and construct the meaning. The word *unexpectedly* will mean not looked out for, something that comes out of the blue.

Student interest in Latin-based words can be increased by pointing out how they are used in J. K. Rowling's *Harry Potter* books to name her characters and as names for charms and spells (Nilsen & Nilsen, 2006). For example, the dark character of Lord Voldemort comes from the Latin word *mort*, which means death. In English, words with *mort* include *mortal, mortuary, morbid, morgue, mortgage* and *martyr*. The spell Petrificus Totalus! is from the Latin word *petra*, or stone, and means freeze, or stop someone. In English, words with *petra* include *petrify* and names such as *Peter, Pita* and *Petra*.

Greek words

In the upper grades of school the pupil will come across many Greek words. Some of these have come into the English language by way of Latin, or they have come into the language because they have been needed for new ideas and concepts in science. Imagine you have just read the title of a story called *Arach-attack*. It is an actual story (Trigwell, 2009). In the story, one of the characters sees a spider and kills it. A line in the story gives some helpful context: "I then studied the corpse of the squashed arachnid on the post and then thought of cleaning it up but decided to leave it there as a warning to other spiders not to mess with me" (p. 20). If you know *arach* is Greek for spider, then the sentence, and the title of the story, makes sense. So it helps to know the meanings of Greek words.

As we saw for Anglo-Saxon words, many Greek words are compounds; for example, *thermometer*, *microscope*, *cardiograph*, *telescope*, *hemisphere* and *arachnophobia*. A clue to recognising Greek words is that they have some unique spellings. In the word *chlorophyll* there are three Greek spellings: the *ch* with a /k/ sound, as in *character*, the *ph* with a /f/ sound as in *photograph* and the *y* with a short /i/ sound as in *gym* and *physics* (Henry, 2003). There are some other distinctive spellings but they don't occur very often, like *pn* (*pneumonia*) pronounced /n/, *mn* (*mnemonic*) pronounced /n/, *rh* (*rhododendron*) pronounced /r/ and *ps* (*psychology*) pronounced /s/.

Summary

Many thousands of words in English are compound words, or are affixed words (they have prefixes and/or suffixes attached to root words). Students can learn many words by breaking them down into familiar meaningful parts rather than learning them as if they are totally new and different structures. Familiarity with a small number of morphemes can help the student to take apart words and then build a meaning for many of them. Structural analysis is not the only way to get to the meanings of words, but even a partial structural analysis, combined with contextual clues, can reveal the meaning of words, so it is an important skill to teach.

There are also some important teaching implications for struggling readers. For one thing, they are likely to learn words better if they see the spellings of words. The teacher who intuitively explains the meaning of a new word, and even illustrates it, is doing exactly the right thing. If the teacher writes the word, and uses phonics to show how to sound it out and pronounce it, this will be significantly better than just talking about the word. There are huge opportunities to do this in shared book reading, where pupils can see the printed word.

The teacher who singles out a list of unfamiliar words a day for attention—especially if it is part of the shared or guided reading lesson, with a focus on spelling and meaning, before reading a shared book story or article—will be doing a lot of good, especially for the poorer readers in the class. Ten words a day, five days a week, for a school year, is 2,000 words a year. If the struggling reader remembers just half those words it will be a huge gain for them. If you then add all the other words pupils will learn just from reading books in class and at home, that adds up to a lot of words. Teaching vocabulary can make a difference!

STRUCTURAL ANALYSIS

Follow-up activities

The activities that follow this chapter are intended to raise student awareness of structural awareness; that is, how words are constructed, and can be deconstructed. The aim is not busy work—we suggest that the teacher review the worksheets with pupils after they are completed, asking them what they learnt, and checking that they understand the concepts of structural analysis; for example, that a compound word is two simple words put together, and that this is a common way to make new words in English.

SAMPLE LESSON

The Wandering Heartbeat

Vicky McCallum, Junior Journal 2001, 23, 7–7.5 years (Reprinted with permission)

My Grandad was really sick. The doctor called an ambulance to take him to the hospital. Grandad needed oxygen to help him breathe. I was scared. I thought Grandad was going to die.

Mum and Dad took me to see Grandad in the hospital. The doctor told us that Grandad's heart wasn't working very well. He had to have a box with some wires on it on his chest. Mum explained that the box was called a telemeter. It's like a remote control for a television except it picks up heart signals. The doctors and nurses used it to check that Grandad's heart was beating properly.

Grandad didn't die. He was in the hospital for a week. It was lucky that he had the telemeter on him. Mum said that the nurses kept losing Grandad in the hospital. He wandered off at three o'clock one morning. They finally found him, but then he disappeared again.

The telemeter was still sending out signals of his heartbeat to the monitor, so even if they didn't know where he was, the nurses knew that he was all right.

Mum saw Grandad's hospital chart the next day. Underneath the printout of his heartbeat, it said, "While wandering". Mum smiled when she told me that.

When Grandad started to feel better, he was allowed to come back home to Nana, but he's got to take it easy from now on. His heart is still weak, and he has to take ten pills every day. He still likes to wander, so Nana's bought him a scooter, but she has to keep an eye on him!

LESSON PLAN

This story is about a boy's Grandad who was taken to hospital because his heart was not beating properly. The story consists of primarily Anglo-Saxon words but also Latin, Greek and French.

A key word in this story is telemeter. It is a Greek word (two combining Greek forms: tele + meter). Comprehension of this story partly depends upon the understanding of the Greek word telemeter.

Connect

Teacher: What do the following words have in common?
[Write the words on the whiteboard.]

        television   *telephone*   *teletext*

Child: They all have tele-.

Teacher: That's right.

[Underline tele- in each word with a red whiteboard marker.]

Let's take a look at the second part of each word.
[Underline the word root -vision, -phone and -text with a blue whiteboard marker.]

Discuss the meaning of each word root:
vision—to see
phone—to hear
text—printed material (provide an example)

Let's take a look at the first part of each word, tele-. What do you think tele- means? Tele- means "at a distance".

In this story you will be reading about a telemeter.

Remember tele- means at a distance.
[Show pupils a metre ruler.]

What does meter mean?
[to measure]

A telemeter measures information and sends it somewhere. In this story a telemeter is used to measure Grandad's heartbeat and then it sends it to a monitor that nurses in the hospital can read.

Let's take a look at another word in the story: *wandering*.

Have you ever sung the song, "I love to go a wandering upon the mountain track. And as I go I love to sing with a knapsack on my back"?

What do you think *wandering* means?

Wander: to walk about in a place, stroll, "cruise"

This story is called *Wandering Heartbeat*. What do you think *wandering* means in this sentence? [the heart is not beating regularly]

Grandad also "wanders" off? What is meant by *wanders* in this sentence? [takes off—but not in a hurry …]

What is a heart? A beat? *Heart + beat = heartbeat*. A heart that beats.

What do you think "wandering heartbeat" means?

WORD ANALYSIS

Anglo-Saxon
Compound words (two Anglo-Saxon words that have been joined together to make one)

	underneath	printout	heartbeat
Latin	ambulance	amulate—move about	
	hospital	"of a guest"; "a host—receiver of guests"	
	remote	move away, to move back—far removed	
	disappeared	appear—come before, come toward to show dis- prefix meaning not	
	monitor	from monere—to warn	
Greek	telemeter	tele—at a distance, far meter—measure.	
	television	tele—at a distance, far vision—to see/sight	
Other French	oxygen		

STRUCTURAL ANALYSIS

Activities

Activity 5.1: Contractions

A contraction is like a compound word. It is where two words are joined together but shortened a bit by taking out one or more letters and replacing them with an apostrophe.

Rule: The apostrophe is placed where the missing letter used to be. For example, it's** means "it is".

Remember: You only put in an apostrophe if a letter is missing. Write contractions for these words. Circle the letter or letters that you leave out when you write the contraction.

Contractions with not	Contractions with is
do not _____	she is _____
was not _____	he is _____
did not _____	**it is _____
cannot _____	that is _____
have not _____	there is _____
Contractions with will	Contractions with have
he will _____	I have _____
I will _____	you have _____
she will _____	we have _____
they will _____	they have _____
we will _____	
you will _____	
Contractions with am	Strange contractions (will → wo)
I am _____	will not _____

** Remember that it's means it is. When you write its without an apostrophe it means possession, such as "My car is due for its warrant of fitness next month."

Activity 5.2: Making new words with different prefixes

Column 1 has some common prefixes. Column 2 has the meanings of the prefixes. These prefixes can be used with real words. Choose a base word from those shown below and put the right prefix on it:

night, social, armed, circle, market, build, portable, legal, pay, marine, behave, honest

Then write the new word in Column 3.

PREFIX	MEANING	WORD WITH PREFIX
un	not	
re	again	
il	not	
dis	not	
mis	not	
sub	under	
pre	before	
super	bigger than normal	
semi	half	
anti	against	
mid	middle	
trans	across	

STRUCTURAL ANALYSIS

Activity 5.3: Greek words

There are many words of Greek origin that have come into the English language. The words are often made up of two parts, each of which is important for working out the meaning of the word, like compound words.

Clues for recognising Greek words

1. CH is pronounced /k/

2. PH is pronounced /f/

3. Y sounds like short i

Greek words can often be broken into two parts that each mean something. For example, photograph is Greek. Photo means "light" and graph means "write". Archaeologist is also Greek. Archaeo means "ancient" and logo means "study". An archaeologist studies old things like ancient pottery that is dug up from under the ground, and so on.

Match the following Greek words to their meanings: **archaeology, microscope, thermometer, psychology, telephone, photograph, telescope**.

Suggestion—use the dictionary to find out what each part of the Greek word means and then match it with the definitions below.

WHAT THE GREEK PARTS OF THE WORD ORIGINALLY MEANT	WHAT IS THE WORD?
seeing something from a distance	
writing with light	
hearing sound from a distance	
study of the mind	
measure of heat	
an instrument for looking at very small things	
study of very old places and things	

Activity 5.4: Greek words

Write meanings for the Greek words below.

GREEK WORDS	MEANINGS
dinosaur (deina means terrible and saur means lizard)	
octopus (octo means eight and pous means feet)	
biography (bio means life)	
autograph (auto means oneself and graph means write)	
psychological (psych means mind and logy means study)	
metropolis (polis means city)	
zoology (zoa means animals)	
Polynesia (poly means many and nesia means islands)	
antibiotic (anti means against and bio means life)	
democracy (demos = people and cracy is government)	
autocracy (auto means one)	
astronomer (aster means star)	
monopolise (mono means one)	
energetic (erg means work)	
physics (phys means nature)	

STRUCTURAL ANALYSIS

Activity 5.5: Which language do these words come from?

Look at this list of words and then write the words in each column according to whether they are Greek, Romance (Latin, French) or Anglo-Saxon.

Clues:

1. The Anglo-Saxon words are compound words—two simple words put together to make a new meaning.
2. The Romance words have a base word like spir and either a prefix, a suffix or both.
3. The Greek words are also compounds. Each half of the word has a meaning but it is not a simple, common word—another clue is to look for Greek spellings like ph (f), ch (k) and y (i) sounds.

	GREEK	**ROMANCE (LATIN OR FRENCH)**	**ANGLO-SAXON**
amphibious commercial realisation retraction mechanism disappear intellectual scholarship underhanded aspiration technology pharmacy uncomfortable birthday popcorn agricultural cartwheel headlights gymnasium motorbike disruption fireplace swordfish palaeontologist			

Activity 5.6: Latin words—Prefixes

Write a sentence that shows the meaning of each word.

PREFIX	MEANING	EXAMPLE	WRITE A SENTENCE
re	again	reconsider	We would like to reconsider your offer.
pre	before	prediction	The weather reporter made a prediction that there will be rain next Friday.
post	after	postpone	The soccer game is postponed because of rain.
sub	under	submarine	
un	not	unbelievable	
uni	one	unicycle	
bi	two	bicycle	
tri	three	tripod	
de	away	departure	
ex	out	expulsion	
mis	wrong	miscalculate	
retro	back	retrospective	
super	above	superannuation	
trans	across	transformation	
pre	before	prediction	
intro	within	introduction	
inter	between	intermingle	
extra	outside	extraordinary	
circum	around	circumference	

STRUCTURAL ANALYSIS

Activity 5.7: Suffixes

Latin -ious words

The suffix -ious changes the word into an adjective, which is a describing word. For example: "That pie is delicious." (Simple meaning is yummy, tasty.)

Look at the words below and write what you think they mean.

LATIN WORD	SIMPLE MEANING
1 He was *gracious* in defeat.	
2 She is a *cautious* traveller.	
3 She is *audacious* in sport.	
4 He is a *pretentious* person.	
5 She buys *ostentatious* cars.	
6 He is a *fractious* person to work with.	
7 He has a *malicious* tongue.	
8 At meetings he is too *loquacious*.	
9 The detective thought the man looked *suspicious*.	
10 The cat looked *supercilious*.	

Activity 5.8: Is this a person?—Suffixes with -ion and -ian

Many words end in -ion or -ian. The secret is to remember that -ian refers to people.

Look at the list of words below and write in the correct ending -ion or -ian.

BASE WORD	SUFFIX -ION OR -IAN?
state	station
magic	magician (a person)
construct	
music	
subtract	
politics	
direct	
electrics	
ignite	
tactics	
tense	
mathematics	
invent	

STRUCTURAL ANALYSIS

Activity 5.9: Making new words

The aim of this activity is to show you that many words in English are made up by adding prefixes and suffixes to the root word.

Challenge!

It has been said that you can make up to 100,000 words from just 12 Latin and Greek root words. They are listed below. Work with a few of your classmates, using a dictionary and thesaurus, to see how many words you can make. Could you make 100,000?

Your task for today is to choose five root words and see how many new words you can make in 10 minutes.

Hint: Use some of the prefixes and suffixes in the exercises above to help you make new words. For example, the Latin root scrib, spript, combined with some prefixes and suffixes, can make words like: prescribe, prescription, prescriptive, inscribe, inscription, describe, description, descriptive, circumscribe, subscribe and so on.

LATIN ROOT	MEANING	EXAMPLE
scrib, script	to write	manuscript, transcribe
spec, spect, spic	to see, watch or observe	spectator, spectacles
mit, miss	to send	missionary, submit
duc, duce, duct	to lead	education, conductor
fac, fact, fect, fic	to make or do	factory, officiate
tend, tens, tent	to stretch or strain	extension, tendon, tension
cap, ceit, ceive, cep, cept, cip	to take, catch, seize, hold or receive	captor, concept, recipient
ten, tain, tin, tinu	to hold	retain, container, detainee
sist, sta, stat, stit	to stand	stamina, station, understand
pon, pose, pound	to put, place or set	deposit, proposal
plic, ply	to fold	duplicate, replicate
fer	to bear or yield	fertilise, reference
Greek combining form		
graph	written or drawn	biography, autograph
ology	science or study of	biology, criminology

CHAPTER 6

Constructing Word Meanings With Concept Maps

Introduction

Constructing word meanings with concept maps takes the student from the known to the unknown, building on what they already know in an organised way. Concept maps help to organise thinking. This chapter will explain four kinds of concept maps that can be used in the classroom:
- web
- weave
- Venn diagram
- thermometer.

Teaching concept maps is made easier by using a model of instruction called CORE. It shows how to connect students' "known" ideas to the "unknown" new vocabulary to be learnt, and it encourages reflection and further learning about the topic. To illustrate how to teach concept maps, the chapter includes two sample lesson plans.

What are vocabulary concept maps?

Vocabulary concept maps are diagrams that visually represent relationships among words and concepts. There are different types of concept maps. Some are complex and some are relatively simple. Vocabulary concept maps are a tool learners of all ages can use to organise and represent information. In this chapter we focus on four vocabulary concept maps: web, weave (or matrix), Venn diagram and thermometer.

Why use concept maps?

According to Calfee and Patrick (1995, p. 95), vocabulary concept maps should be used because they:

> begin[s] with student knowledge and experience, and build[s] on this base in an organised way. Asking students 'What comes to mind when you think about *dogs*?' is more authentic than 'What is a dog?' The range of possible answers is more varied and more informative, and the semantic web provides a framework for portraying the responses.

Vocabulary concept maps, as a vocabulary tool, give students a more precise understanding of words. They also help students to organise and categorise words and concepts and provide a context for learning new vocabulary. As

Calfee and Patrick (1995, p. 96) put it, "webs and weaves allow students to make effective use of what they already know, but they can also be tools for helping students see what they *need* to know and how to organize information they find in other sources".

The CORE model of instruction

The CORE model of instruction (Connect, Organise, Reflect and Extend) provides a framework for lesson design (Calfee & Patrick, 1995; Dymock & Nicholson, 2007). The CORE model (see Figure 6.1) begins by connecting students to the topic using questions that promote thinking and discussion. Asking the right questions is a key characteristic of the model. The organise stage of the model is when the concept map is developed. Concept maps should be large enough for students to see (we will look at some examples shortly). Whiteboards, smart boards, overhead projectors or large sheets of paper are all appropriate for concept maps. The reflect stage provides an opportunity to return to the concept map and discussion and reflect on the content and structure. During the reflect stage students should be encouraged to step back and reflect on the lesson. The extend stage includes activities that promote extension and transfer of learning. Extension is an opportunity for meaningful practice.

FIGURE 6.1: THE CORE MODEL OF INSTRUCTION

```
            Connect
            engage
             play
  Extend              Organise
  apply   INSTRUCTION structure
  transfer            reconstruct
            Reflect
           look back
            explain
            critique
```

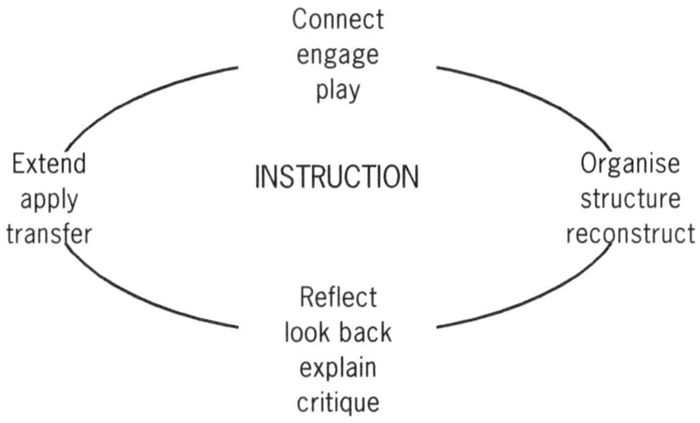

Source: Calfee & Patrick, 1995, p. 63

Vocabulary concept map 1: Webbing

Description

What is webbing? Webbing (some refer to webbing as semantic mapping) is when students brainstorm a word (or topic) (e.g., rugby, Auckland, apples, mammals, transport, natural disasters) and organise the words into categories. Webbing has this name because it is like a spider web (Calfee & Patrick, 1995). A spider web has a centre and a number of fine threads that form a network of lines. A key point to remember about webbing is that it is about *one* thing, *one* topic. This is the centre of the web. The threads from the centre (or main topic) link to subtopics. The diagram below of a spider web illustrates this centre and the lines that extend from the centre.

FIGURE 6.2: THE SPIDER WEB IS THE CONCEPTUAL BASIS FOR WEBBING

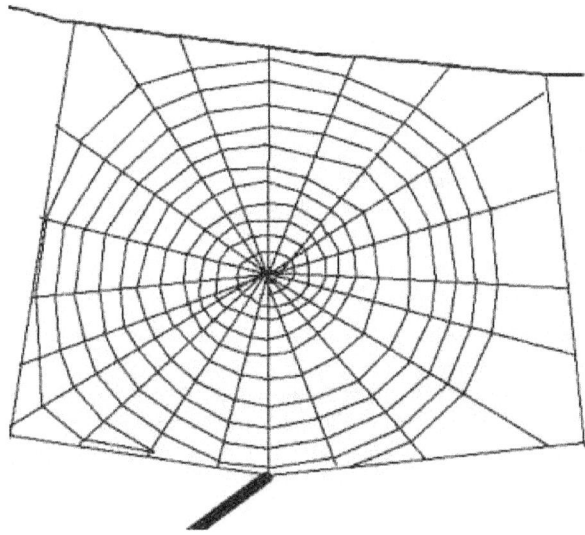

Figure 6.3 shows a webbing diagram a student or teacher could use for information about a word relating to a concept (e.g., friendship or loneliness) or topic (e.g., Wellington, New York, fish or natural disasters). Figure 6.3 could be used for Auckland city.

FIGURE 6.3: EXAMPLE OF A WEB BLANK, CENTRING ON THE WORD AUCKLAND

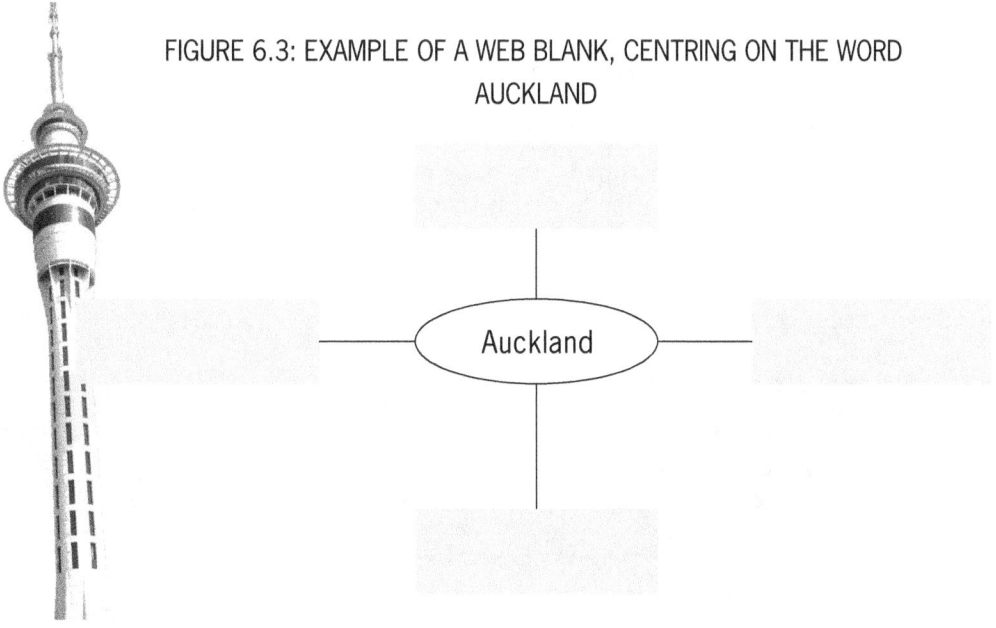

CONSTRUCTING WORD MEANINGS WITH CONCEPT MAPS

SAMPLE WEBBING LESSON

Topic: Hens

Year level: Year 3 or Year 4

Resource: "Happy Hens", Pat Quinn, *School Journal*, Part 1, Number 3, 1997

Learning objectives: By the end of this lesson children are expected to have an understanding of:

- how to identify/classify categories for groups of words associated with the word *hen*
- how to identify/classify categories for groups of words associated with the word *birds*.

Literacy learning progressions (Ministry of Education, 2010 p. 14): By the end of Year 3 students are expected to include "increasingly specific" vocabulary in their writing. Students are also expected to be aware that common words have multiple meanings (e.g., *bank, point*).

Lesson sequence (based on the CORE model of instruction)

Background

"Happy Hens" is an article about a Wairarapa family that raises free-range poultry. The article describes the daily life of free-range hens. It also describes the role of the family in looking after the hens. This article could be used in a unit on birds, eggs, hens, farming (particularly organic), different types of jobs or lifestyles. The article is at a 7.5–8 years reading age and is written primarily for Years 3 and 4 children.

Connect

Teacher: Today we will be reading an article called "Happy Hens". Before we read the article we are going to brainstorm what we know about the word *hen*. What comes to your mind when you hear or read the word *hen*? What does *hen* make you think of?

Children: A bird. A bird that lays eggs for us to eat. Birds in small cages. I have seen birds in small cages on the news.

Teacher: You are right. A hen is a bird. Here is a picture of a hen.

Organise (free generation and classification)

Teacher: A hen is a special type of bird. I am going to put the word *hen* in the middle of the whiteboard. Let's see how many words or phrases we can think of that are associated with the word *hen*. You have already mentioned cages, bird and eggs. What else can you think of? (Note: group the words in categories.)

Children: A hen is quite large for a bird. It has feathers and wings. They don't fly much. Nest. Not all hens live in cages. Some hens roam free. Poultry. Hen house. Brown. Cackle. Beak. Sharp claws.

Teacher: Well done. I have grouped your responses into three groups. Let's look at the first group of words. What could be a heading for this group? (See completed web in Figure 6.4.) (The words are *cage* and *henhouse*.)

Child: Cage and henhouse are types of homes for the hen.

Teacher: Great. I will put types of homes as a heading. (Continue with the other two groups—physical features and characteristics.)

FIGURE 6.4: A COMPLETED WEB FOR HENS

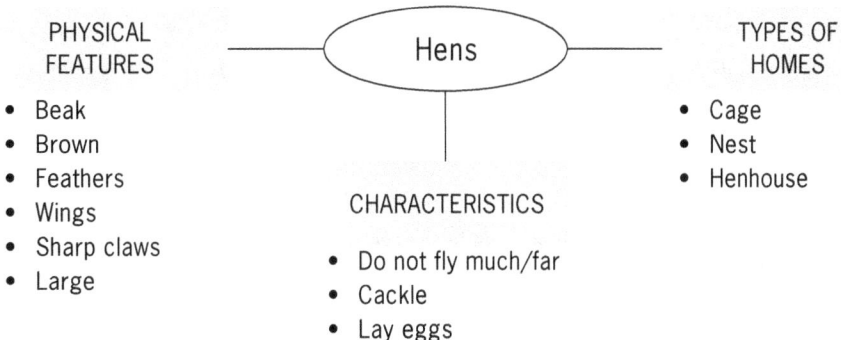

PHYSICAL FEATURES
- Beak
- Brown
- Feathers
- Wings
- Sharp claws
- Large

CHARACTERISTICS
- Do not fly much/far
- Cackle
- Lay eggs

TYPES OF HOMES
- Cage
- Nest
- Henhouse

Teacher: I would like to take this discussion on hens a bit further. A hen is one type of bird but as you know there are other types of birds. What other types of birds do you know? Think about birds you have seen in your garden, or in the park or on television. I will write the names of the birds on the whiteboard as you name them (see Figure 6.5).

FIGURE 6.5: A WEB FOR TYPES OF BIRDS—NO LABELS

- Hen
- Chicken
- Ostrich
- Rooster

- Penguin
- Albatross
- Mallard
- Pelican
- Stork

- Duck
- Goose
- Blackbird
- Starling
- Swan
- Thrush

- Kiwi
- Bellbird
- Tui
- Kakapo
- Kaka
- Fantail
- Saddleback
- Morepork
- Kea

- Hawk
- Eagle
- Falcon

- Kiwi
- Penguin

- Duck
- Pheasant
- Quail

- Owl
- Morepork

TEACHING READING VOCABULARY

CONSTRUCTING WORD MEANINGS WITH CONCEPT MAPS

Teacher: Excellent. You will see that I have arranged the words in a particular way. Why do you think I have put *kiwi*, *tui*, *fantail*, *bellbird*, *kakapo*, etc. together? (Teachers' note: Calfee and Patrick, 1995, refer to this as "classification".)

Child: Because they are New Zealand native birds. A hen is not a native bird so it is not in that group.

Teacher: Excellent. What does *native bird* mean?

Child: Kiwi and tui are found only in New Zealand. You will not see a kiwi in another country. I think native means just here in New Zealand. Each country has animals that are special to them. Like the koala is an Australian animal. And raccoon is an American animal.

Teacher: Let's look at another group of birds. Why do you think *ducks*, *blackbird*, *starling*, *swan* and *thrush* are grouped together?

Child: We have starlings in our backyard. We have blackbirds. When we go to the park we feed the ducks. The heading could be *birds close to home*.

Continue discussion completing labels for the web. Discuss alternative labels. For example "birds close to home" could be "city birds". (See Figure 6.6.)

FIGURE 6.6: COMPLETED WEB FOR TYPES OF BIRDS—WITH LABELS

Reflect

What have we learnt about hens? What have we learnt about types of birds? How did we categorise the birds? Why didn't we put the penguin and hen in the same category?

Extend

Have students search the Internet for images of the birds using Google Images. The images could be printed and labelled, and children in small groups could quiz each other. Students may have heard of tui, fantail and starling, but may not be able to identify the birds.

Students individually, in pairs or in small groups could think of other birds to add to the web.

Note: It is not unusual practice to brainstorm children's responses to words and to record their responses so the group or class can see. For example, a Year 5 class may be focusing on sports. The teacher begins the discussion by putting *rugby* in the middle of the whiteboard. The teacher asks children to share what comes to mind when they think of rugby. The teacher then writes their responses on the board. The board may look something like this (see Figure 6.7).

FIGURE 6.7: AN EXAMPLE OF CHILDREN'S RESPONSES TO WHAT COMES TO MIND WHEN THEY THINK OF RUGBY

Colin Meads   strength   tall
    rugby ball   fast
goal kicks   goal posts
scrum   **Rugby**
                Daniel
mouth guard   passing   Carter
line outs   scrum machine   commitment
Jonah Lomu   head gear   practice

For some students this brainstorm may be a sea of words. They are unable to bring coherence out of chaos. Webbing will bring structure to this sea of words. With the rugby brainstorm you could ask students if they can see common themes or categories. From this sea of words you could put the brainstorm into a vocabulary web (see Figure 6.8). We recommend teaching students how to categorise as the brainstorm progresses (as shown in Figure 6.5) or after the brainstorm (as shown in Figure 6.8).

FIGURE 6.8: A RUGBY WEB

Famous players — RUGBY — Rugby moves
Player features — RUGBY — Equipment

Concept map 2: Matrix/weave

The matrix or weave is an extension of the web. The matrix provides an opportunity for students to compare and contrast concepts. Calfee and Patrick (1995, p. 68) explain that "Weaves are matrices, the crosshatch of cells providing opportunities for comparisons and contrasts." The weave might be used to compare two feelings (e.g., happy and sad), three types of bears (e.g., black, polar, brown) or four cities (e.g., Auckland, Hamilton, Wellington and Christchurch). The matrix below shows how rugby and cricket can be compared and contrasted.

FIGURE 6.9: AN EXAMPLE OF A MATRIX USING TWO SPORTS

	Rugby	Cricket
Equipment		
Famous players		
Moves		
Player features		
Season		
Clothing		

Matrix (weave) lesson

Topic: Bicycles (transport)

Year level: Upper primary/intermediate

Resources: There are a number of *School Journal* articles that would be suitable for a unit on bicycles (Table 6.1).

TABLE 6.1: SOURCES FOR A MATRIX/WEAVE LESSON ON BICYCLES

TITLE	AUTHOR	JOURNAL	READING AGE	SUBJECT
"Bicycle Courier Wanted"	Solveig Mikkelsen	P4N3 1995	9.5–10.5	Wellington cycle courier
"Mountain Bike Accident"	Norman Bilbrough	P4N2 1994	9–10	Mountain bike rider's bike accident
"Pumping the Pedals"	Maggie Lilleby	P4N3 2004	10–12	BMX racing
"You Can't Ride That!"	Joy Graham	P3N3 2004	9–10	Bike riding in 1898—improper for girls to ride a bike
"Calling All Riders!"	Michelle Osment	P1N3 2008	9–10	Preparing for a BMX race
"Making Tracks"	Phillipa Werry	P3N1 2001	9.5–10.5	Developing a mountain bike park

Learning objectives: By the end of this lesson children are expected to have an understanding of the complexity of bicycles, different types of bicycles, what they are designed for, their characteristics, number of gears and who rides the bikes.

In *The Literacy Learning Progressions* the Ministry of Education (2010, p. 16) states that by the end of Year 6 students should be able to "draw on knowledge and skills that include selecting vocabulary that is appropriate to the topic, register and purpose (e.g., academic and subject-specific vocabulary appropriate for specific learning areas."

Lesson sequence (based on the CORE model of instruction: Calfee & Patrick, 1995; Dymock & Nicholson, 2007)

Background

A Years 6–7 class is studying transport, with a particular focus on bicycles. Several students have recently competed in the November Lake Taupo Cycle Challenge and two students participated in the Meridian Kids Bike Jam earlier in the year. Discussion reveals that the bikes they rode in the two events were quite different. This leads to a further discussion on various modes of transport, but the main focus of the discussion is on the many types of bikes available. Due to the children's interest in bikes, their teacher prepares a reading unit on bikes. This unit also links to the class science topic on sustainability and the environment.

Connect

Teacher: Over the next two weeks we are going to be reading a number of articles about bikes. *Bike* is the informal way of saying *bicycle*, which is formal. Do you know what the word *bicycle* means? (Greek origin. From Late Latin *cyclus*, from Greek *kuklos*, wheel; *bi* from Latin, from *bi*—twice, having two.)

There are many types of bicycles just like there are different types of cars. Some cars are built for speed (racing cars) while others are built to carry people (family cars). What I would like you to do is turn to your neighbour and have a chat about bicycles. Talk to your neighbour about the different types of bicycles.

Organise

What are some bicycles types? (See Figure 6.10). As you identify the different types of bicycles I will list them on the board. (Brainstorm: list bicycle types on whiteboard.)

FIGURE 6.10: BRAINSTORMING BICYCLE TYPES

BMX	Tandem
Trail	Road racing
Track racing	Mountain
Children	Touring

Teacher: Well done. Let's think about what each bike is designed for. A BMX bike has a particular purpose and a mountain bike has a different purpose. What is the BMX bike designed for? Tandem? Trail? (Record responses.)

What are the characteristics of the BMX bike? If you were to describe the BMX bike to someone who has never seen it, what words would you use? (Complete for each bike type.)

What would another subtopic be? We have bicycle types, what the bikes are designed for and characteristics. What could another subtopic be? (Figure 6.11 is a completed weave.)

CONSTRUCTING WORD MEANINGS WITH CONCEPT MAPS

FIGURE 6.11: A COMPLETED WEAVE FOR BICYCLES

BICYCLE TYPES	DESIGNED FOR	CHARACTERISTICS	GEARS	WHO RIDES THE BIKE
BMX	Racing Dirt riding Just for fun Wheelies Jump Acrobatics	1 gear Hand brakes (usually) Knobbly tyres Not a large bike Small wheels	1	Younger (school age)
Tandem	Touring Racing 2 riders	2 riders Big and hard to transport	1–27	Generally older riders
Trail	Trail and road	Like mountain bikes but not as rugged	21–24	High school students Commuters Family riding
Road racing	Speed Roads	Lightweight frames Little accessories Dropped handlebars Narrow tyres	14–27	14–35 years
Track racing	Speed Tracks	Simple Lightweight No brakes		15–30 years
Mountain	Mountain trails Cross country (places a normal bike can't go)	Flat handlebar—as high as or higher than seat Wide tyres	15+ Some gears are low for steep hills	Riders who want an off-road experience 10 years+
Touring	Touring—long rides	Durable Comfortable Good for long journeys Can carry packs		
Exercise	Exercise	Stationary		Gym Home use

Reflect

Why did we organise the information in a weave or matrix?

Extend

Students could complete the gaps. An advantage of the weave is that gaps are clearly evident. Students could add another subtopic to the weave, or another type of bike.

Concept map 3: Venn diagram

The Venn diagram (Calfee & Patrick, 1995, p. 95) is "like a matrix, the diagram shows how two topics are alike and different". Venn diagrams can be used to show similarities and differences between two concepts. Similarities are recorded in the overlapping section of the diagram and the differences are in the nonintersecting sections. The Venn diagram, like the web and weave, is an excellent tool for discussion. We recommend teachers use the Venn diagram when comparing and contrasting two concepts/words, particularly when you want to focus on similarities and differences. Figure 6.12 shows the similarities and differences for teddy bears (stuffed) and brown bears (real).

FIGURE 6.12: VENN DIAGRAM FOR TEDDY AND BROWN BEARS

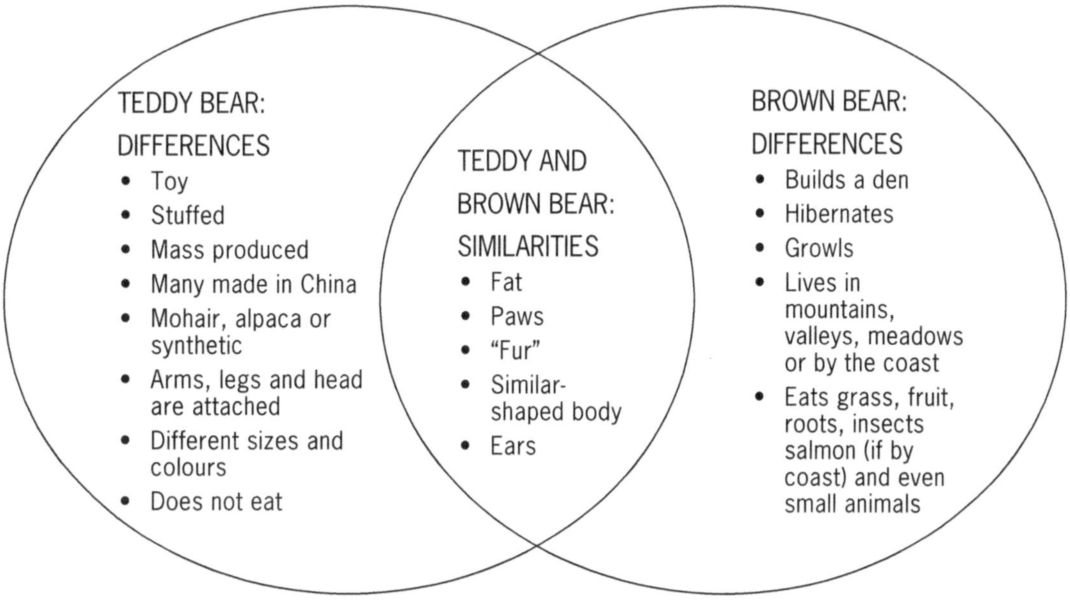

TEDDY BEAR: DIFFERENCES
- Toy
- Stuffed
- Mass produced
- Many made in China
- Mohair, alpaca or synthetic
- Arms, legs and head are attached
- Different sizes and colours
- Does not eat

TEDDY AND BROWN BEAR: SIMILARITIES
- Fat
- Paws
- "Fur"
- Similar-shaped body
- Ears

BROWN BEAR: DIFFERENCES
- Builds a den
- Hibernates
- Growls
- Lives in mountains, valleys, meadows or by the coast
- Eats grass, fruit, roots, insects salmon (if by coast) and even small animals

Concept map 4: Thermometer

The thermometer "uses a familiar metaphor to introduce students to precise work usage" (Calfee & Patrick, 1995 p. 95.). The thermometer provides students with an opportunity to categorise or rank words.

Linking with the unit on bicycles, the teacher could ask students how they feel after a long bike ride or, for some, how they felt after completing the Taupo Cycle Challenge (see Figure 6.13). Students could write their word on post-it stickers and place it according to value (high/low) on the chart. Or the teacher could record the words on the board ("word splash") and then together categorise the words according to how they feel after a long bike ride:

CONSTRUCTING WORD MEANINGS WITH CONCEPT MAPS

FIGURE 6.13: A WORD SPLASH OF WORDS DESCRIBING HOW THE PUPILS FELT AFTER A LONG BIKE RIDE

```
HOW I FEEL AFTER A LONG BIKE RIDE

              energetic              jaded
   weary   ok   beat    bushed    active
      exhausted fatigued   lively
   worn-out   vigorous              sleepy
           lethargic    drained
```

A possible ranking for the word splash could look like this (see Figure 6.14). Rankings will vary from class to class, group to group and rider to rider.

FIGURE 6.14: A THERMOMETER FOR WORDS DESCRIBING FEELINGS AFTER A LONG BIKE RIDE

Thermometer:	Feelings after a long bike ride:
	energetic [+]
	vigorous
	lively
	active
	OK
	sleepy
	weary
	lethargic
	beat
	bushed
	drained
	worn-out
	jaded
	fatigued
	exhausted [–]

Web, weave, Venn diagram and thermometer examples stemming from "The Wandering Heartbeat" (McCallum, 2001)

"The Wandering Heartbeat" (McCallum, 2001) is a *Junior Journal* story about Grandad, who is taken to the hospital in an ambulance due to heart problems. The web, weave, Venn diagram and thermometer could all be used to extend vocabulary before, during or after reading the story. Children could create a web for the word *sick* (see Figure 6.15). *Sick* is a common word, yet how often do we explore the concepts associated with the word *sick*?

FIGURE 6.15: WEB FOR THE WORD *SICK*

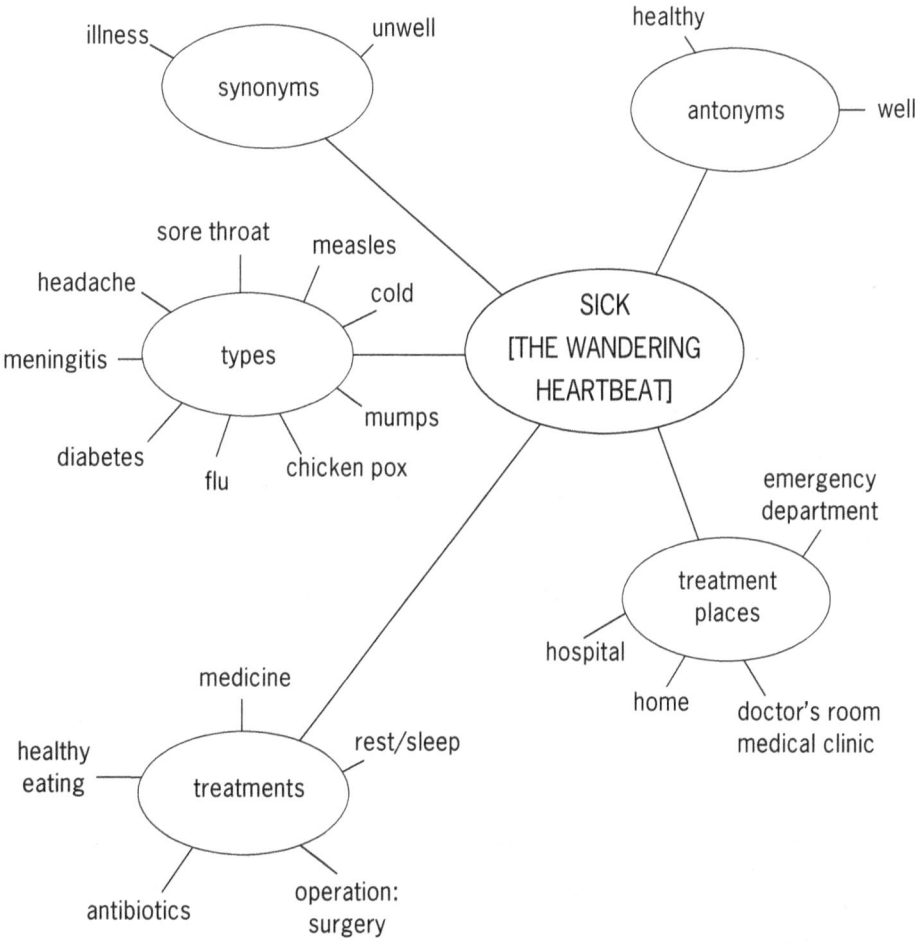

CONSTRUCTING WORD MEANINGS WITH CONCEPT MAPS

Grandad is taken to hospital by ambulance. A matrix could be used to compare and contrast vehicles in terms of their purpose, size, colour and who rides in the vehicle (see Figure 6.16).

FIGURE 6.16: MATRIX FOR MOTOR VEHICLES

	PURPOSE	SIZE	WHO RIDES?	COLOUR
Ambulance	Takes injured or sick people to the hospital	Large	Driver Assistant Injured or sick x 2	White Red
Car	Transports people	Small, medium or large	Driver 1–7 passengers	Many colours
Fire truck	Firemen: help with car accidents and emergencies Carries firemen to fire	Large	Firemen	Red
Police car	Can move very fast Transports policemen	Large	Police: often 2 Criminals going to the police station	White Yellow Blue
Bus	Transports a large number of people	Medium and large	Driver Passengers: up to 50	Many colours
Van	Transports a small group of people	Large	Driver Passengers: 10	Many colours

A Venn diagram could be used to explore the similarities and differences between a hospital and the local medical centre, as shown in Figure 6.17. While conceptually a hospital and medical centre are similar (i.e., both care for people who are unwell), there are many differences (e.g., visiting the medical centre to see the travel doctor in preparation for an overseas trip).

FIGURE 6.17: VENN DIAGRAM FOR HOSPITAL AND MEDICAL CENTRE

HOSPITAL: DIFFERENCES
- Major surgery
- High-tech specialist equipment (e.g., MRI)
- Specialist doctors (e.g., surgeons, consultants)
- Specialist treatment (e.g., radiography)
- Sleep overnight
- Intensive care
- Babies born (maternity)

HOSPITAL AND MEDICAL CENTRE: SIMILARITIES
- Prescribe medicine
- Receive medical treatment
- Doctors and nurses

MEDICAL CENTRE: DIFFERENCES
- GPs
- Health checks
- Immunisation
- Travel doctors
- Treats minor ailments such as colds, flus, minor cuts

A thermometer could be used for the word *scared* (see Figure 6.18). Children may become scared when a family member is taken by ambulance to the hospital. Remember: thermometers will vary from child to child, or group to group.

FIGURE 6.18: THERMOMETER FOR THE WORD *SCARED*

Thermometer:	for scared (most scared to least):
	petrified
	terrified, terrorised
	scared
	frightened
	fearful, fear
	panicked
	afraid
	troubled
	alarmed
	startled
	nervous
	timid
	anxious

Summary

This chapter has shown how it is possible to explain the meanings of many words by linking them with other meanings, looking at their features (webbing), comparing and contrasting them with other words (weaves), showing how they share some features of other words but not all features (Venn diagrams) and showing how words can be graded on a continuum that links synonyms and antonyms (thermometer). The nice thing about these mapping strategies is that they take the student out from the word, showing how the word links with what they already know, and encourage them to make links to new words that they do not know but are related to the words they do want to know. Concept maps help students to learn "subject-specific" vocabulary which is one of the aims of the *Literacy Learning Progressions* (Ministry of Education, 2010), that by the end of Year 6 it is expected that students will use "academic and subject-specific vocabulary" p. 16)

CHAPTER 7

Exploring the Multiple Meanings of Words

Introduction

An important part of building up a meaningful vocabulary is being able to make connections among words. For example, some meanings can be expressed by more than one word. These words are synonyms. Other words can be connected because they are opposite to each other. These are antonyms.

Another important part of building a vocabulary is to make connections within words. This can be done by studying the etymology of words: what language they came from and what they originally meant. It can also be done by looking at the internal structure of words, to see if there are familiar, meaningful parts that can help us to get to the meaning.

Exploring the multiple meanings of words can be a lot of fun. There is much humour in English that is due to the multiple meanings of words. For example, each week, the *New Zealand Listener* has a column that is a lot of fun to read because writers forget that words have multiple meanings. The column consists of snippets taken from newspapers around the country, from Internet advertising and so on. Here are some examples (Life in New Zealand, 2010, 28 February, 20 March and 3 April):

- Pot plants relieve stress (www.stuff.co.nz, 17/3/10)
- In fact, the Queen doesn't even turn up tour national day. She doesn't even send her Willie. (*The Press*, 6/2/10)
- The atmosphere in Wellington was electric, Mr Laker said, "The town's chock-full of AC/DC fans ..." (*Southland Times*, 21/1/10)
- Glutton free organic cake (sign at a Wellington airport café)

Why explore the multiple meanings of words?

Is this part of the reading and writing standards?

The answer is *yes*. Learning that words have multiple meanings, that they can be ambiguous and that some phrases do not mean literally what they say—like metaphors and similes—are things that school-age children are expected to handle. The reading and writing standards for Years 1 to 8 (Ministry of Education, 2009) state that pupils in Year 3 will be reading words with multiple meanings, and that by Year 4 they will be reading ambiguous words and figurative language, like metaphors and similes.

The importance of learning words through talking, reading, spelling and writing

We suggested in Chapter 5 that the best way to learn new word meanings is to build up as many associations as possible: to read, spell, say, hear how they are used, discuss and define them, so that they make sense and pupils know how to use them in meaningful ways. This strategy also applies to words that have more than one meaning. The strategy is to make glue-like connections between the meanings of words and their form.

The strategy also applies to words, phrases or expressions with a figurative meaning; that is, when they take on a new meaning when they cross word boundaries in unexpected or unusual ways, such as metaphors, similes, jokes, idioms and proverbs.

Multiple meanings are the building blocks of a rich vocabulary

Teaching about the multiple meanings of words involves teaching pupils how to have a set for diversity when they think about the meanings of words. It is important because so many words have multiple meanings. Johnson, Moe, and Baumann (1983) reported a study of 9,000 of the most frequently occurring words in English, in which they found that more than seven out of 10 words were polysemous; that is, they had multiple meanings. For example, *bat* is a polysemous word. If someone says, "There's a bat in the attic", is it a baseball bat or an animal? Either meaning is possible. It is important to be aware of the double meanings of many words so that you are not confused.

The different ways in which words are polysemous

The word *polysemous* comes from Greek. *Poly* means many and *sem* refers to meaning, so *polysemous* means having many meanings. For example, many words are homonyms, they are spelt the same but have different meanings. For example, the word *good* can have more than one meaning. There is a difference between a *good* book (interesting) and a *good* meal (delicious). In this case, the meaning of the word changes but has the same germ of meaning. Other times the meaning seems to change a lot; for example, *smoke* in "She likes to smoke a pipe" and "She likes to smoke fish". Sometimes the meaning of the word changes totally; for example, as in *bank*, a place to put money, and *bank*, the side of a river. The word *run* can have many meanings: a run in cricket, a run of bad luck, to give someone a run for their money, a run on the bank, a run-in with an enemy, run out of steam, take the car for a run, a run-down house and so on.

EXPLORING THE MULTIPLE MEANINGS OF WORDS

Then there are homophones, words that sound the same but are spelt differently. Many students can get them confused as was the case in the 2010 New Zealand Spelling Bee. The newspaper report of the Spelling Bee noted that "it paid to know your homonyms—for instance acquiesce* and aqueous* could easily be your undoing" (Donaldson, 2010). Our focus in the chapter will be on these sorts of words, where the meanings of certain words and phrases can trip you up.

Then there are homographs, meanings that are spelt the same but are pronounced differently, such as *bass* the fish and *bass* the musical instrument (or singer with a low voice).

Homophones

Homophones are words that are pronounced the same but differ in their spelling. Some writers say that homophones drive their students crazy (Tompkins & Blanchfield, 2008). Homophones can certainly be very annoying. Imagine you are a sign writer and you have spent an hour painting a sign that reads, "No cars *passed* this gate!", and some eight-year-old on her bicycle stops at the sign and says, "Hey, mister, you've made a spelling mistake! It should be *p-a-s-t*."

The main thing to remember about homophones is that they are pairs or triplets of words that sound the same but are spelt differently and have different meanings. It is a good idea to teach homophones by using written examples. It is a good thing to do because research indicates that learning the spellings of new words as we learn their meanings helps to cement those meanings into memory (see Chapter 5). Simply saying the words and not writing them for pupils to see can be confusing, like the old story of the children at church who heard the words in the hymn "*the cross I'd bear*" as "*the cross-eyed bear*". It is much better to write each word in the homophone pair. Knowing the spellings of homophones is not just helpful for reading but for writing as well. A computer's spell checker will allow words that are real words, but will also allow misspelt homophones because they are real words too (Yopp & McAdams, 2007). For example, this sentence sailed through the spell checker: "A paragraph could have miner floors but wood bee past by a spell checker."

Teachers usually teach their pupils the obvious problematic homophones, such as *to/two/too*, *there/their*, *no/know*, *it's/its*, *whose/who's*, *I/eye*, *see/sea* and *right/write*, but there are many other homophone pairs and triplets that could be covered. The aim of a homophone lesson is to bring to the attention of the class that although homophones sound the same they can have totally different meanings, so you have to be careful in case you get confused.

The fact that homophones sound the same but have different meanings has enabled writers to write humorous books, like: *A Chocolate Moose for Dinner* (Gwynne, 1976); *The King Who Rained* (Gwynne, 1970); *A Little Pigeon Toad* (Gwynne, 1988); *What in the World is a Homophone?* (Presson, 2005); *How Much Can a Bare Bear Bear?* (Cleary, 2005); *Eight Ate: A Feast of Homonym Riddles* (Terban, 2007). Such books are humorous because the printed word gives one meaning while the illustration shows the other meaning.

Tompkins and Blanchfield (2008) suggest teaching a class unit on homophones where pupils collaborate to make a class book. On each page of the book pupils write the homophone pairs, use each word in a sentence and illustrate each word as well. For example, with *sword/soared*, the word *soared* could have a sentence plus an illustration of superman soaring into the sky, and *sword* another sentence to explain the word, and an illustration of a knight with a sword in hand.

Homographs

Homographs, like *bass* and *bass*, *row* and *row*, *desert* and *desert*, are spelt the same but differ in their meaning and pronunciation. The main thing to remember is that even though the spelling is the same, the words are pronounced differently, so this is the clue to their meaning. Johnson and Pearson (1984) suggest a matching activity to encourage pupils to understand homographs. Pupils have to draw a line from the sentence to the matching definition:

| The police are following a new *lead*. | metal |
| The *lead* pipe was heavy. | clue |

Alternatively, pupils can create sentences that contain the homographs:

| I wonder if the rubbish truck will *refuse* to take our *refuse* if the bin is too full. |
| The Council will not *permit* you to own a gun without a *permit*. |
| The rock star will *record* her new album soon and it is sure to be a *record* hit. |
| I won't *read* the paper until I have *read* the book. |
| Maths is my best *subject* but I won't *subject* you to it unless you are interested. |

Another idea is to practise the different ways that homographs are pronounced. The different pronunciations are usually because the two meanings are different in tense or are different parts of speech; for example, *refuse* is a verb and *refuse* is a noun. To raise awareness of the different way to pronounce homographs, give students some sentences and they will have to read them aloud the way they are pronounced.

TABLE 7.1: DISTINGUISHING THE MEANINGS OF HOMOGRAPHS

HOMOGRAPH	MEANING
I *object* to taking a bus to school because it takes too long.	opposed to, protest
The *object* of this activity is to help you win the next netball game.	aim

Homonyms

Homonyms, like *bark* and *bark*, *club* and *club*, are spelt the same and pronounced the same but differ completely in meaning. Teachers can raise awareness of the different meanings by encouraging students to link sentences that contain homonyms to their meanings.

TABLE 7.2: DISTINGUISHING THE MEANINGS OF HOMONYMS

HOMONYM	MEANING
The letter is in the *post*.	mail
We dug a *post* into the ground.	pole

In this chapter we describe homonyms as instances where the meaning of the same word changes totally; for example, as in *bank*, a place to put money, and *bank*, the side of a river. We will not look at cases where the same word has several different meanings depending on context but the word can still seem to have the same underlying idea. For example, *hot* can change its meaning, as in hot dog, hot car, hot band, hot on the trail, hot spicy food and hot pink, but there is still a sense of positive temperature. There are many variances of meaning of the word *bad*, but most of them have the sense of "not good" as in bad weather, bad feeling, bad cold, bad news, bad person, bad day and bad meal. These are definite changes of meaning but the germ of the meaning stays the same. We will not cover this type of change in this chapter.

Figurative language

It has been estimated that adults use over 500,000 figures of speech a year, though most of them are clichés (Petrosky, 1980). One way of thinking about figures of speech is that we are not supposed to take them literally. They are different kinds of *metaphors*.

Metaphor

Metaphors use words in unusual ways to attract our attention. They are a creative way to express an idea. There is often a clash of meanings, but the metaphor works in that we think of a situation, idea or person in a different way. The words in a metaphor are not meant to be taken literally. The definition of *metaphor* is an implied comparison between an idea and something that has a similar meaning, but in an unusual way; for example, *blinded by love* (can't think rationally), or *my salad days when I was green in judgement* (my youth). School-age pupils can appreciate metaphors; for example, that a word like *cool* can have a metaphorical meaning that is not its literal meaning, such as a *cool* reception.

Metaphors can be very simple, such as *foot of a mountain, lip of a pot, bridge of a nose, coat of paint, eye of the hurricane, blanket of clouds, star of the show, caught red-handed*. You can also mix your metaphors, for example: "If you play your cards right you'll hit the bullseye"; "She weighed up the arguments carefully to see if they would hold water." A mixed metaphor can work well if it is done deliberately for humorous effect and the reader can see that it is, but in a lot of writing metaphors are mixed unintentionally, and this is not regarded as good writing.

Simile

A simile is an explicit comparison using *as* and *like* to link two words or phrases, where you are not meant to take the expression literally but to treat it as a comparison; in other words, there are similarities between the two things. For example, *swears like a trooper, eats like a horse, runs like the wind, as plain as the nose on your face*.

Many similes are clichés—worn-out, over-used expressions—such as *thick as thieves, neat as a pin, fit as a fiddle, as white as snow, easy as pie, quiet as a mouse, happy as a clam* and *easy as falling off a log*.

Idioms

A broad definition of *idiom* is that it is the way people talk, like the language of lawyers, politicians and scientists. They seem to talk differently from us. For example, if there is a simple word to use, lawyers often seem to resist this and choose a more arcane expression.

This more general definition of idiomatic speech is not what we are talking about here. In this chapter we are concerned with multiple meanings of words and expressions and this is another way in which we use the term *idiom*, to refer to expressions that do not literally mean what they say. They do not even metaphorically mean what they say. In a metaphor, there is some way to get meaning; for example, *steely eyes* has a sense of eyes that are hard and unfeeling. With idioms, you are unable to make these links. For example, the idiom *to kick the bucket* means *to die* but there is no way to get *die* out of *kick* and *bucket*.

It is tempting to ignore idioms as just an unfortunate blip on the grammatical landscape of language but there are thousands of idioms in English, just as many as adjectives, so we do need to attend to them (Jackendoff, 2002).

Grammatically they are stored in our mental lexicon, our mental dictionary, in the same way as words. They probably started off once upon a time as sentences but their deep structures, their meanings, have been frozen. Most of the time, we can't treat them like sentences, and change them like we can change other sentences. For example, "The bucket has been kicked by John" is different from "John has kicked the bucket", so we store them like words, each with their own particular meaning (Jackendoff, 2002).

Someone learning a new language can be totally confused by idioms because they do not literally mean what they say. For example, in English, when you are invited to someone's house and asked to *bring a plate*, this does not literally mean to bring an empty plate. The *Amelia Bedelia* books by Peggy Parish (1963) give humorous illustrations of idioms that Amelia gets wrong. For example, when Amelia was told to *draw the drapes*, she got out her pencils and drew a picture of the drapes (Blachowicz & Fisher, 2002).

Idioms can usually be boiled down to a one- or two-word meaning, like *pay through the nose* (expensive), *down in the dumps* (sad), *the jig is up* (caught out), *that's the way the cookie crumbles* (bad luck), and *not out of the woods yet* (still struggling) (Baumann & Kame'enui, 2004). There are some easy, off-the-shelf idioms that everyone knows, like *eat humble pie* (apologise), *spit it out* (talk) and *fly off the handle* (lose temper).

Some idioms are technically like metaphors in that they are extending a meaning to another area of meaning. For example, *let the cat out of the bag*, where "the cat" is a secret, or *the line must be drawn somewhere*, where "the line" is a distinction, whereas "the bucket" in *kick the bucket* does not have that kind of metaphorical meaning (Jackendoff, 2002).

Yet the above idioms are not metaphors in the traditional sense in that they are well-known expressions. Traditionally, the definition of *metaphor* is a creative, different way of expressing an idea, usually with an obvious semantic clash, to make speech or writing more interesting and impacting (Jackendoff, 2002). An example would be from Shakespeare's *Antony and Cleopatra*, "those were my salad days when I was green in judgement".

Idioms are expressions that are learnt separately from the words they are made up of. For example, the expression, *raining cats and dogs* has a different meaning from its literal meaning. It does have the sense of heavy rain, but why cats and dogs? No one is exactly sure how we store idiomatic meanings in our mental dictionary, but it is worth teaching about idioms because they do occur quite a lot in language (Jackendoff, 2002).

Proverbs

These expressions are also like metaphors, but have a different purpose. The *Oxford Dictionary* defines a proverb as "A short, pithy saying in general use, held to embody a general truth". Their meanings are more than the sum of the words in them. Some examples of proverbs are *familiarity breeds contempt, haste makes waste, strike while the iron is hot* and *still waters run deep.*

Jokes and puns

Learning about the multiple meanings of words is a big step towards having a sophisticated understanding of language. Many jokes play on the different meanings of words—these are called puns. Students can appreciate jokes that contain puns much better if they have this set for diversity; for example, "boo" in the following:

    Knock, knock.

    Who's there?

    Boo.

    Boo who?

    No need to cry, it's only a joke.

They will appreciate other jokes, like: "Why did the student take her car to school?—To drive the teacher up the wall." They will also appreciate the use of pseudohomophones like, "This chicken is very eggspensive."

Summary

Teaching about the multiple meanings of words helps to improve children's vocabulary learning by adding more detail and precision to their understanding of words. Students who understand that even familiar words can have multiple meanings will have a set for diversity, so that when they are reading or listening they will not be confused.

We should also try to involve students in lots of reading activities that clarify multiple meanings because reading will give lots of contextual clues, and it will also provide the correct spellings of words, which in turn acts like glue to cement the different meanings. This is especially the case with homophones. Their different spellings will stick to the correct meaning and make it easier to recall which meaning is correct.

The multiple meanings of many words will be learnt by reading in context and by wide reading, but we strongly recommend also giving some instruction for students in your reading class. The suggestions we have recommended can be taught successfully in many classrooms.

Exploring the Multiple Meanings of Words

Activities

Activity 7.1: Understanding homophones

Homophones are words that sound the same but are spelt differently and have different meanings, such as *great* and *grate*. Read each context clue below and put a circle around the correct homophone that fits the meaning of the sentence.

CONTEXT CLUE	HOMOPHONES	
These are grown in the garden	carats	carrots
When you don't want something	know	no
What you have left if you buy 10 oranges and eat two of them	eight	ate
It eats grass and has long ears	hair	hare
When your throat is sore and you can hardly speak	hoarse	horse
You need this to bake a cake	flower	flour
They are passed down from parent to child	genes	jeans
A ruler who is leader of a country will do this	rain	reign
You can put this in the ground to support the beanstalk as it grows	steak	stake
This is a very strong metal used in cars	steal	steel
You have five of these on each foot	toe	tow
It is a sea food	muscle	mussel

Activity 7.2: Homophone hink-pinks

Homophones are words that sound the same but are spelt differently and have different meanings, such as *great* and *grate*. Hink-pinks are two words that rhyme but also have a funny meaning. Write a sentence that describes what each hink-pink means. For example, *a bare bear is a bear with no clothes on*. Suggestion: use your dictionary.

HINK-PINK	MEANING
a bare bear	a bear with no clothes on
a berry bury	a berry that has died
a bored board	
a callous callus	
a scent cent	
a chilly chili	
a dough doe	
a not knot	
a lone loan	
a maize maze	
a mined mind	
a muscle mussel	
a pale pail	
a hoarse horse	
a night knight	
a plain plane	
prince prints	
a profit prophet	
a roll role	
stationary stationery	
a steel steal	
a towed toad	
a weight wait	
a weak week	
a sail sale	
a Sunday sundae	

EXPLORING THE MULTIPLE MEANINGS OF WORDS

Activity 7.3: Homophones—can you tell the difference?

Homophones are words that sound the same but are spelt differently and have different meanings, such as *great* and *grate*. In Column 2 the homophones are used in sentences. Fill in the blank spaces with the correct homophone from Column 1 for each sentence. You may need to check the meanings with your dictionary.

HOMOPHONES	MEANINGS
stairs, stares	I can't stand the _____ that I get when I go to the beach.
	I walked up the _____ to the second floor.
road, rode	Timothy _____ his bicycle down the country _____.
allowed, aloud	The children were not _____ to shout _____ in school.
mail, male	Our pet cat is a _____.
	Our dog chases the postie when she delivers our _____.
blew, blue	There was a lovely _____ sky but the wind nearly _____ us over as we walked down the street.
sun, son	The mother spoke sternly to her _____ to tell him not to go out in the _____ without a hat.
boar, bore	A _____ is someone who is uninteresting and makes you want to go to sleep.
	A _____ is a wild pig.
stationary, stationery	The _____ shop did not just sell paper, but magazines and books as well.
	The bus was _____. It had not moved from the bus stop because it was waiting for a new driver.

Activity 7.4: Homophones—can you tell the difference?

Homophones are words that sound the same but are spelt differently and have different meanings, such as *great* and *grate*. In Column 2 the homophones in Column 1 are used in sentences. Fill in the blank spaces with the correct homophone for each sentence. You may need to check the meanings with your dictionary.

HOMOPHONES	MEANINGS
role, roll	I had a _____ in a play. I was one of the main characters.
	I ate a bread _____ with egg on it for lunch.
bear, bare	The cupboard was _____. There was no food at all.
	The _____ climbed up the tree.
minor, miner	The _____ went down into the coal mine.
	It was a _____ accident, hardly a dent in the car.
guerrilla, gorilla	A _____ is a type of soldier.
	A _____ is a large animal in the jungle.
rap, wrap	I bought the present but then I had to _____ it.
	The band played _____ music.
fair, fare	We had to pay a $20 _____ for the ferry ride but it was a _____ price because the trip took an hour.
compliment, complement	When the teacher says "good job", it is a _____ to the pupil.
	We do not have to fight because our stores _____ each other. They sell shoes and we sell socks.

EXPLORING THE MULTIPLE MEANINGS OF WORDS

Activity 7.5: Homographs—can you tell the difference?

Homographs are words that are spelt the same but are pronounced differently, and have different meanings, such as *bass* (pronounced "bass") and *bass* (pronounced "base"). In the following lists, draw a line from the sentence to the correct meaning.

HOMOGRAPH		**MEANING**	
1	The police are following a new *lead*.	1	metal
2	The *lead* pipe was heavy.	2	clue
3	It was hard to *polish* the car.	3	make bright and shiny
4	Our teacher is *Polish*.	4	comes from Poland
5	There is a *tear* in your jacket.	5	fluid from the eye
6	I cried a *tear* of happiness.	6	rip
7	The farmer went to *sow* barley.	7	plant seeds in the ground
8	The *sow* had a litter of piglets.	8	adult female pig
9	It is hard to tie laces into a *bow*.	9	front part
10	The *bow* of the boat needs repair.	10	knot
11	I can *row* the boat.	11	argument
12	The two friends had a *row*.	12	pull the oars

Activity 7.6: Homographs—practise reading them aloud

Homographs are words that are spelt the same but are pronounced differently, and have different meanings, such as *bass* and *bass*. In the following lists:

- draw a line from the homograph in Column 1 to its meaning in Column 2
- choose someone to read to.

Your task is to read each homograph with the correct pronunciation. Then your partner will read to you.

HOMOGRAPH		MEANING
1	I *object* to taking a bus to school because it takes too long.	aim
2	The *object* of this activity is to help you win the next netball game.	opposed to, protest
3	Liam will present his project to the class.	in attendance
4	Is Liam *present* in class today?	explain
5	The essay is good but the *content* is weak.	substance
6	I'm happy and *content* to be a teenager.	satisfied
7	This town is like a *desert*.	give you up; abandon
8	I won't *desert* you.	empty space
9	She was gone for nearly a *minute*.	60 seconds
10	An ant is a *minute* insect.	very small
11	There was a picture of a *bass* on the wall.	musical instrument that plays a low sound
12	She plays *bass* at school practice.	fish

EXPLORING THE MULTIPLE MEANINGS OF WORDS

Activity 7.7: Homonyms

Homonyms are words that are spelt and pronounced the same but have different meanings, such as *trunk* and *trunk*. Write two possible meanings for each homonym in Column 1. For example, a *top* can mean a spinning toy or the summit of a mountain. You will need to use a dictionary.

HOMONYM	**MEANING 1**	**MEANING 2**
top	a toy that spins	the top of a mountain
mine		
bar		
dull		
green		
line		
bank		
note		
strong		
knock		
power		
sink		
sharp		
bark		
club		

Activity 7.8: More homonyms

Homonyms are words that are spelt and pronounced the same but have different meanings, such as *trunk* and *trunk*. Each homonym in Column 1 has two meanings. In Columns 2 and 3 write a sentence using each meaning. Also draw a picture of each meaning if you can.

HOMONYM	SENTENCE 1	SENTENCE 2
pen		
fly		
note		
school		
post		
bat		
train		
cross		
watch		
spring		
crack		

EXPLORING THE MULTIPLE MEANINGS OF WORDS

Activity 7.9: Even more homonyms

Homonyms are words that are spelt and pronounced the same but have different meanings, such as *trunk* and *trunk*. In the following lists, draw a line from the homonym to its meaning. After you do this, write in your Reading Book your own new sentences for each homonym.

HOMONYM	MEANING
The letter is in the *post*.	pole
We dug a *post* into the ground.	mail
The *star* twinkled.	famous
She is a movie *star*.	a large bright ball of gas in the sky
The elephant's *trunk* is for drinking.	long nose
The clothes are in a *trunk*.	box with a lid
This is a walking *club*.	a stick with a round head for hitting a ball
This golf *club* cost a lot of money.	group of people with a special interest
The tree is losing its *bark*.	short, loud noise
Our dog likes to *bark* at passing cars.	tough skin of a tree
My bike is *green*.	jealous
He was *green* with envy.	colour

Activity 7.10: Idioms

Idioms are expressions that can usually be boiled down to one or two words.

In the following lists, draw a line from the idiom to its meaning.

IDIOM	MEANING
down in the dumps	in trouble
drop in the bucket	not concentrating
not out of the woods yet	give a false warning of danger
in one ear and out the other	small amount
cry wolf	sad
in a pickle	act very carefully so as not to upset someone
walk on egg shells	still obstacles to overcome
given the cold shoulder	not wanted
blow the whistle	told off
turn over a new leaf	accomplice
cat's paw	tell tales
read the riot act	make a fresh start
over the moon	big fuss about a small matter
bite the dust	happy
storm in a teacup	disintegrate, die

EXPLORING THE MULTIPLE MEANINGS OF WORDS

Activity 7.11: Proverbs

The *Oxford Dictionary* defines a proverb as "A short, pithy saying in general use, held to embody a general truth". It is a saying that expresses an idea that many people think is true.

Write sentences that explain the meaning of these proverbs.

	PROVERB	SENTENCE
1	the more the merrier	
2	the squeaky wheel gets the grease	
3	a bird in the hand is worth two in the bush	
4	you can't make an omelette without breaking eggs	
5	a leopard can't change its spots	
6	rats desert a sinking ship	
7	the early bird catches the worm	
8	an elephant never forgets	
9	make hay while the sun shines	
10	after the storm the calm	
11	silence is golden	
12	time is money	
13	better a patch than a hole	
14	necessity is the mother of invention	

Activity 7.12: Simple metaphors

A metaphor is a creative, different way of expressing an idea, where you use a word in an unusual way, to make speech or writing more interesting and impacting.

Read the metaphors below, put a circle around the metaphorical word and write down what you think the metaphor means.

METAPHOR	MEANING
foot of a mountain	base of the mountain
lip of a pot	
bridge of a nose	
coat of paint	
eye of a hurricane	
blanket of clouds	
star of the show	
legs of a chair	
roof of the mouth	
shoulder of the road	
spearhead a campaign	

EXPLORING THE MULTIPLE MEANINGS OF WORDS

Activity 7.13: Similes

A simile is where you compare one thing with another using *like* or *as*. A simile is different from a metaphor because a metaphor does not use *like* or *as*.

The similes below are called "off the shelf" because they get used a lot, but they are useful to know.

Can you guess the word that is at the end of each simile below?

To help you, the missing words are in Column 2.

	SIMILE	MISSING WORD
1	This material is as smooth as _____.	snow
2	The room was as black as _____.	bone
3	The dress was as white as _____.	rose
4	This bed is as hard as a _____.	pin
5	After going all day without water, I am as dry as a _____.	log
6	This 1970 car is as old as the _____.	elephant
7	Their garden is as neat as a _____.	jackrabbit
8	Those gossips are as thick as _____.	bee
9	Cooking scones is as easy as falling off a _____.	mud
10	This message is as plain as the nose on your _____.	thieves
11	This textbook is as clear as _____.	pigsty
12	She is up and down like a _____.	face
13	A memory like an _____.	rock
14	Fly like a butterfly, sting like a _____.	silk
15	He smelt like a _____.	hills
16	Your room looks like a _____.	night

CHAPTER 8

The Dictionary and Thesaurus

Introduction

The dictionary and thesaurus are highly under-used ways of improving children's vocabulary. Together, they are the "holy grail" of vocabulary learning. They are both a gold mine of information but they are very different. They are organised in different ways. If you want to find out what a word like *osprey* means then you need to go to a dictionary. A thesaurus is different. If you want to find a synonym—a word that has a similar meaning—then you go to a thesaurus.

In this chapter we will suggest that the dictionary and thesaurus are vital tools for word learning but that they must be combined with context clues from reading or from listening. In isolation, the dictionary and thesaurus are not sufficient. An example of this is in the movie, "Boy", where the main character is told by the school principal that he has *potential*. The boy looks up the word in the dictionary and it says "having the capacity to develop into something in the future: *a potential problem*". That is not what the principal meant, of course, and that is why the dictionary is not the total answer to learning words. It is helpful but it is not an island. It has to be combined with reading, listening and discussion.

Do our students use the dictionary and thesaurus?

One reason why we think it is so important to get students excited about the dictionary and thesaurus is that many pupils do not seem to like using them, even though these resources are often available in class. They are available but the problem is that they are usually sitting in a corner, ignored, like wall flowers at a dance. We will later explain why pupils really need to treat the dictionary and thesaurus as their best friends but for now we accept that pupils find it hard to make friends with these valuable resources.

We say this because we conducted a survey of a class of Years 4–5 students and asked them two questions: "How do you feel when you have to look up a word in a dictionary?" and "How do you feel when you have to look up a word in the thesaurus?" We asked the pupils to circle one of five puppies, and to write about their feelings.

We were surprised at how many pupils circled the unhappy puppy. Some comments on using the dictionary were:

> Some of the dictinorys don't have the word.
>
> It is alright but sometimes it gets really annoying to find a word.
>
> It's boring and hard to find words.
>
> Becose some times I cont find my word.
>
> Because you have to go back and forth!
>
> Because it is not fun and takes forever to find my word.

Some comments on using a thesaurus were:

> Hard to find words.
>
> I don't really like the thesaurus.

On the positive side, some pupils said about the dictionary, "It's kind of fun", "You learn new words and also get the meaning" and "I love learning about new words because I like to learn the meaning but sometimes I'm too tired." There were also positive comments about the thesaurus, such as "They have more words for that one word and it is interesting to see what other words there are" and "It's nice and easy to find a discriptive word."

The dictionary

When we think back to our discussion of the history of the English language in Chapter 1, it is interesting that English, by the end of the 1500s, had grown to nearly 200,000 words, yet there were not any dictionaries for people to use (Winchester, 2003). No one had come up with the idea of a dictionary in the way we know it today; that is, a list of English words in alphabetical order, with each word's meaning listed, as well as a guide to how to pronounce the word, and where the word came from.

This situation was soon to change. A number of English dictionaries were printed in the 1600s (Balmuth, 2009), but the one that became most famous and most influential in terms of later dictionaries was Samuel Johnson's *Dictionary of the English Language*, which was published in 1755. Winchester (2003) described Johnson as "the bookseller's son from Lichfield in Staffordshire, the schoolteacher turned journalist and parliamentary sketch writer and wanderer and conversationalist who would become one of the towering figures of English letters" (p. 27). Johnson's dictionary stayed in print for over 100 years—it was a classic. It only had 43,500 words, which was nowhere near the total of English words at that time, but it was more than enough. A really helpful feature of the dictionary was that Dr Johnson included quotations to illustrate how to use words. This dictionary became a blueprint for later dictionaries.

One of the reasons people liked Samuel Johnson's dictionary was that the definitions were interesting to read. For example, he famously defined the word *oats* as "a grain, which in England is generally given to horses, but in Scotland supports the people". When we read that definition nowadays, it seems to be a bit light-hearted; that is, an Englishman making fun of the Scots. On the other hand, at the time he wrote the definition, maybe he was not joking. Certainly oats, in the form of porridge, was long a staple in Scotland. And the English did not have a very high opinion of the Scots.

In America, the equivalent to Samuel Johnson as a writer of dictionaries was Noah Webster, who published his *American Dictionary of the English Language* in 1828 (Henry, 2003). Winchester (2003) described the dictionary as "formidable" and Webster as "the 'short, pale, smug and boastful' schoolmaster from New Hartford, Connecticut" (p. 33). Webster was already well known for his spelling book that sold many millions of copies. Webster's dictionary had 70,000 words, many more words than Johnson's dictionary, and became *the* dictionary. Webster is famous for simplifying some of the spellings of English words, which is why American spellings nowadays are sometimes different from our own; for example, *color* instead of *colour*, *realize* instead of *realise* and so on.

This was not the end. The task of collating, defining and finding illustrative quotations showing the use of the hundreds of thousands of words in English was taken on by the English Philological Society. It took 70 years and culminated in the publication of the *Oxford English Dictionary* (OED) in 1928, defining more than 400,000 words. And the task is still going. The 1989 second edition of the OED defined 615,000 words, and showed the use of the words with 2,436,000 quotations. The dictionary is in 20 volumes, has 59 million words and 21,730 pages. It is also available online. The story of the OED is described by Simon Winchester in a book titled, *The Meaning of Everything* (2003).

The point is, though, that dictionaries are interesting to read. Some people love dictionaries. They are fascinating, especially if they have the etymologies of words; that is, their histories, where they come from. They are essential for any writer and for spelling as well. You can become addicted to dictionaries; for example, there is a recent book published about someone who spent a whole year reading the OED. It is called *Reading the OED: One Man, One Year, 21,730 Pages* (Shea, 2008). Each chapter is a letter of the alphabet and at the end of each chapter the writer gives a list of interesting words starting with that letter. For the letter *A*, for example, there is *avidulous* which means "somewhat greedy" but not excessively so. For the letter *B* there is *bed-swerver*, referring to an unfaithful spouse. Anyone who enjoys dictionaries will like this book.

How dictionary writers write their definitions

A dictionary writer (lexicographer) usually uses the system of "genus-plus-differentiae" (Calfee & Associates, 1984). The genus is the superordinate of the word (the category that includes this word and others like it). The differentiae are: (1) functional difference; (2) difference in appearance; and (3) subclass. These are the features of the word that make it different from others. The dictionary definition will follow this basic pattern:

> **(Target word)** is a **(genus)** for/that/to **(differentiae)**
>
> A definition may focus on difference in *appearance*:
>
> *pony* is a horse that is small

or a difference in *function*:

> *saunter* is to walk slowly and casually
>
> *retina* is the light-sensitive part at the back of your eyeball that receives an image and sends it to your brain
>
> *screwdriver* is a tool for turning screws
>
> *liquorice* is a root of a plant to flavour sweets

or a difference in *subclass* (e.g., male/female):

> *heroine* is a character in a book, film or play who is female
>
> *hen* is a chicken that is female.

If–then definitions

Sometimes the definition will describe an if–then situation in which the word can be explained:

> *fault*—if something bad is your fault, then you are to blame for it; if you are at fault, then you are mistaken, or to blame for something.

Two-step definitions

Sometimes a definition will not follow the pattern exactly in that it will use a synonym, or similar-meaning word, which you then have to look up as well to make the pattern. For example, a *mallet* is described as a hammer (you then have to look up *hammer*) and a *mere* is described as a weapon (you then have to look up *weapon*):

> *weapon* is an object that is used to kill or hurt people in a fight or war.
>
> *mere* is a Māori weapon that is flat, like a club, made of greenstone.

Other parts of the definition: Part of speech, pronunciation and word origin

The definition of a word will give its part of speech and its pronunciation. For example, the dictionary may say that the meaning of *ricochet* is when an object or projectile hits a surface at an angle and then bounces off it. For part of speech it may say that *ricochet* can be a noun or a verb. For pronunciation the dictionary may break *ricochet* into syllables and say that it is pronounced *rick-oe-shay* or *rick-osh-ay*. If the dictionary includes etymologies, or word origins, then it may also tell you what language the word comes from, such as Old English (Anglo-Saxon), Latin, French or Greek. In the case of *ricochet*, a clue to its origin is that in French words the *ch* is pronounced as /sh/. The word *ricochet* comes from the French language. It may also give examples of the word used in a sentence context.

How to look up a word in a dictionary: What pupils need to know

We mainly use a dictionary to find definitions of words. The words in an ordinary dictionary are listed alphabetically, so the student needs to be able to spell. It is pointless asking students to look a word up in a dictionary unless they can spell. (Note that there are special dictionaries for pupils who can't spell, and these would be useful for pupils who have these difficulties—for example Moseley, 2001.)

It is also important to have an understanding of alphabetical order to use the dictionary; to know, for example, that the letter *f* comes before *g*, the letter *s* comes before *t* and so on. Once you know alphabetical order you can tackle the dictionary. To be able to look up a word in the dictionary you will need to know alphabetical order, sometimes to the third, fourth, fifth or even sixth letters; for example, in order to distinguish between *intervene* and *interrupt*.

At the top of each page of the dictionary is a clue word that tells you if you are getting close to the word. For example, imagine your class is reading an article called "Faulty Vision" (*Orbit—The School Magazine*, 2008, pp. 16–18), and some of the students wonder what the word *faulty* means. So they look it up in the dictionary. They flick through the pages of the dictionary, *a-b-c-d-e*, and then home in on words starting with *f*.

The second letter of *faulty* is *a*, so they turn more pages looking for words that start with *fa*. They keep turning pages until coming to a page that has a clue word, *father*, at the top of the page it is on. This is a clue to say that you are close to finding the target word *faulty*. Then, checking what is on that page, they come to the word *fault*. This is not *faulty*, but it is the base word.

THE DICTIONARY AND THESAURUS

The dictionary describes *fault* as a failing, a blunder, a mistake. It also explains the part of speech: that *fault* can be a verb or a noun. There is a guide to how to pronounce it (*fawlt*). Looking down the list of words related to *fault*, such as *faulted* and *faultless*, the pupil comes to *faulty*. The part of speech of the target word *faulty* is explained as an adjective. The dictionary might explain *faulty* by giving a synonym, hoping you will know the meaning of the synonym. If you don't know the synonym, then you are in a two-step situation. You will then have to look up the meaning of the synonym. For example, *faulty* might be explained in the dictionary as *imperfect* or *wrong*.

There may also be some information about the origin of the word; that is, its etymology. Some dictionaries do not have this feature, but we think etymology is very important as a kind of glue to hold words in memory. If you can locate such a dictionary for your class it would be much better to use. In the case of *faulty*, the dictionary might mention that it was once a French word, *faute*, meaning blemish, failure or offence. We use a similar French expression today, *faux pas*, meaning a false step, a blunder, an indiscretion that might cause offence.

It is worth keeping these criteria in mind when selecting a dictionary among the many that confront you when you go to a bookshop. Here are the criteria:
- Does the dictionary have clear, easy-to-read print?
- Does the dictionary give the part of speech of the word?
- Does the dictionary give a pronunciation guide?
- Does the dictionary give a definition?
- Does the dictionary give the origin of the word; that is, what language it comes from?
- Does the dictionary give an illustrative context that shows how the word is used in a sentence?
- Does the dictionary show other words that come from this word?
- Does the dictionary give some similar words with the same meaning; that is, some synonyms?

Some school dictionaries meet these criteria, but they may not always use all the criteria for each word. Younger students could use the *Collins New Zealand School Dictionary* and older students the *Compact Oxford English Dictionary for Students* both published by Harper Collins, though the *Compact Oxford* is more for high school and university students. A recommended American dictionary that might be used as a link between children's and adult dictionaries is *Merriam-Webster's Intermediate Dictionary* published by Merriam-Webster. Students can also use an online dictionary.

There are some interesting books that can be used in the classroom to bring alive some of these concepts, such as synonyms and antonyms, word origins and so on. Some titles are *Word Origins* (Beal, 2000), *Stop and Go, Yes and No. What is an Antonym?* (Cleary, 2006), *If you were a Synonym* (Dahl, 2007), *Opposites* (Crowther, 2005) and *If you were an Antonym* (Loewen, 2007).

Putting words back into context

It is one thing to look up the meaning of a word in the dictionary; it is quite another to know how to use it in a sentence. The good thing about reading is that if you come to a new word while reading, it is in a context and you can use contextual clues. Using both contextual clues and the dictionary are a powerful way to get a full understanding of unfamiliar words.

The thesaurus

The originator of the thesaurus was Peter Roget, who was born in 1779 and died in 1869. He was a great scholar, who organised the vocabulary of English into a great number of categories and ideas. In the first part of the thesaurus, words were grouped according to categories, such as "birds". In the second part of the thesaurus, all the words in the first part were listed in alphabetical order. You could look up a word in the alphabetical section and then find the page where that word fitted a category. In that category were other similar words, or synonyms.

A modern thesaurus is still called a thesaurus but it is basically a dictionary of synonyms. For example, if you look up *bite* as a verb, you get synonyms like *crunch*, *gnaw*, *munch* and *nibble*. As a noun, you get *nip*, *sting* and *wound*. The important quality the modern school thesaurus has is its ease of use. You just look up the word, as in a dictionary, and it gives you a range of synonyms for that word. It is very user friendly.

The term *thesaurus* comes from the Greek language, meaning a treasure house. It really is a treasure house of words. The thesaurus is an amazing source of synonyms; that is, other words that have similar meanings. It does not seem to be used as much as the dictionary is, but it is a great source of words when you are looking for a word that is a bit different from the one you are thinking of, or when you are looking for an opposite meaning, or antonym, or when you just want to get an idea of what the word means by looking up its synonyms. An example of a modern school thesaurus would be the *New Zealand School Thesaurus* published by Oxford University Press.

The thesaurus is a valuable tool for speaking and writing. It helps you to find better words to use than the usual old tired phrases like *a really good book*.

For example, a school thesaurus is likely to have several other words you can use for *really*, such as a *truly good book* or a *genuinely good book*. One indicator of how important the thesaurus is for writing is that computer word processing programs, such as Word, have a thesaurus built into them.

Synonyms

The thesaurus is the place to find synonyms (words with similar meanings) and antonyms (words with opposite meanings). The reason we need a thesaurus is that the English language, as a result of borrowing so many words from other languages, has many words that have a similar meaning but are not exactly the same.

One reason for so many synonyms in English is that there are two faces to words. For a start, they have a *denotative* meaning, which is the formal definition of a word; for example, *corrupt* means to act dishonestly or illegally in return for money or power. The word comes from the Latin root, *rupt*, which means broken. Words can also have a *connotative* meaning, which includes the emotional and experiential associations we have with the word; for example, *corrupt* has emotional meanings attached to it such as people's feeling that a corrupt person is morally bad or evil. In the thesaurus there are words that have a simlar meaning and also have this connotation, such as *crooked*, *dishonest*, *shady* and *shonky*.

Another reason there are so many synonyms in English is that the denotative meanings of many words (the dictionary meaning) overlap with other word meanings. This overlap is called synonymy (same meaning). For example, *car*, *truck* and *wagon* all overlap in meaning in that they are vehicles of transport, but they are also different. Likewise, *couch* and *sofa* overlap a lot but they are different in formality.

What attributes do these words share: *lamp*, *lantern*, *candle*, *beacon*? Yes, they all generate light.

The thesaurus is also useful when the dictionary definition is not crystal clear. The dictionary can give a clue to the target word, in that most definitions link the target word to a more commonly known synonym, or category, along with the purpose of the target word, and perhaps provide an example of it. A *sarcophagus* might be defined as a stone coffin that is used as a monument for a dead person. And what is a monument? The thesaurus might not have *sarcophagus* but it may have some synonyms for *monument*, such as *gravestone*, *mausoleum* or *tombstone*, so it can help you to get a better idea of what *sarcophagus* means.

Antonyms

The thesaurus can also clarify the meaning of a word by giving words that have the opposite meaning. Two words can be opposite to each other yet still share a basic meaning. For example, *enormous* and *tiny* both refer to size except that one is big and the other is small. For example, the opposite of *relaxed* is *tense*: both are feelings, but one is strained and the other is loose. The antonym for *love* is *hate*. They are both feelings, but one is negative and one is positive.

Some words can have several opposites that may be a little bit opposite or very opposite. For example, the opposite of *elated* is *depressed*, but then *depressed* can have a number of synonyms as well which are also somewhat opposite in meaning to *elated*, such as *despondent*, *glum* and *morose*.

Some words, though, can have only one opposite. For example, the opposite of *dead* is *alive*. There is no in-between meaning, though you could have synonyms for *alive*, such as *breathing* or *animate*. There is the old expression, "You are either dead or alive. If you are alive, make the most of it." Or, you could say, "If you are breathing or animate, make the most of it." The point is that a thesaurus is a useful way to get a broader understanding of a word by thinking about other words that are similar and opposite in meaning.

Summary

Dictionaries and thesauri are fantastic resources and we want students to think so too. To make the dictionary an interesting resource for pupils it is a good idea to give them a reason for looking up words. The best reason is if the words are in the story or article or book they are reading, and if it will help them to understand the text better if they know the meanings of the words. But there can be other good reasons as well, such as looking for words that are grouped around a theme, or that have come into English from other languages, such as Spanish, French, Latin, Greek and Māori. This is what we have tried to do in the activities that follow. The activities are not busy work. They are designed to give students an awareness of what the dictionary and thesaurus can do; that is, how they can strengthen their knowledge of words and expand their capacity to express themselves orally or in writing. Ideas for some of the activities come from Funk and Funk (1958), Henry (2003), Johnson and Pearson (1984), Moats (2000), and Wagner and Wagner (1961).

THE DICTIONARY AND THESAURUS

Activities

Activity 8.1: Using the dictionary and contextual clues

What is the author trying to say? Read the sentences below. Each sentence has a word that is in bold. Look in your dictionary or thesaurus and find a word that fits the sentence and has a similar meaning and write it above the word.

1. Leon watched the woman **shamble** along the rows of tables.

2. He leaned on the counter, flicking absently at a **meandering** fly.

3. Jamie waited until he was alone in the kitchen, then gently **prised** the fridge door open with his fingers.

4. She's talkative and **tedious** and her manners are terrible! She's annoying and bossy and an utter nuisance.

5. Said the wind to the sun, "I can carry off kites and howl down the chimney on **blustery** nights."

6. "Who is that speaking?" asked the surprised fox. "A **ravenous** crocodile who dotes on fresh fox chops, that's who!"

7. "Emily, did you eat the chocolate cake?" Everyone looked at Emily. If she **admitted** it now, she would be admitting to being a liar.

8. Gilbert looked **despondently** at Julian.

9. Somewhere in the house there was a clock with a **smug** smile on its face knowing the trouble it was causing and feeling very pleased about it.

10. She crawled under the tin shed and **scurried** forward on her hands and knees.

11. I then studied the corpse of the squashed **arachnid** on the post.

12. And that was when I saw it. Eight beady, **iridescent**, yellow eyes. Then an assortment of long, fat, furry legs.

Activity 8.2: Using the dictionary—animal groups

Some of the group names are unusual, such as a swarm of bees. Can you find in your dictionary the missing animal names below and write them in?

A shoal of _____

A colony of _____

A flock of _____

A gaggle of _____

A herd of _____

A litter of _____

A pod of _____

A pride of _____

THE DICTIONARY AND THESAURUS

Activity 8.3: Using the dictionary—types of stones

If you were covering your driveway with stones you could choose different types. Can you find in your dictionary what these stones look like and whether they would be suitable in the garden or in the driveway? Write a description of each type of stone next to the word. For example: Gems—precious stones. They would look good in a driveway but it would need a lot of them and it would be very expensive.

boulders—large rocks would not look good in the driveway because they are too big.

cobbles _____

pebbles _____

rocks _____

gravel _____

scree _____

shingle _____

gems _____

Activity 8.4: Using the dictionary—kinds of houses

We all live in a house, but different houses are built in different ways. If you built a house like some of those listed below, how would you describe them, and where would you be likely to find them? For example, a whare is the Māori word for a house, and you would find it on a marae, and whare wānaanga is the word for a house of learning, that could be a library or a university. Use your dictionary to help find out the answers, then write them in.

bungalow—a one-storey house. You would find it in a town or city.

chalet _____

cottage _____

hut _____

igloo _____

bach _____

mansion _____

manse _____

presbytery _____

shack _____

terrace house _____

whare _____

whare wānanga _____

Activity 8.5: Using the dictionary—phobia words

Many words have *phobia* in them. The word *phobia* comes from the Greek language.

What do the *phobia* words in Column 1 mean? Can you match them to words in Column 2?

PHOBIA WORDS	PHOBIA MEANINGS
arachnophobia	fear of colours
ichthyophobia	fear of circles
scriptophobia	fear of foreigners
agoraphobia	fear of water
claustrophobia	fear of spiders
hydrophobia	fear of public places
cyclophobia	fear of fish
xenophobia	fear of small spaces
chromophobia	fear of writing

Activity 8.6: Using the dictionary—tired words

Some words get used too much, like *sad*, *mad* and *happy*. They are called tired words because they get used all the time. Can you look up the meanings of the list of words below and then put a √ into the columns Happy, Sad and Mad/Angry.

LIST OF WORDS	HAPPY	SAD	MAD/ANGRY
jubilant			
woebegone			
irate			
blissful			
doleful			
livid			
euphoric			
lugubrious			
wrathful			
ecstatic			
dismal			
indignant			

THE DICTIONARY AND THESAURUS

Activity 8.7: Using the dictionary—borrowed words

Many words in English have been borrowed from other languages. The words below come from Greek, Latin, French, Spanish, Portuguese, German and Māori.

Choose from the meanings below and write them into Column 2:

- space satellite
- a beetle-like insect that is a household pest
- fluid made from sour wine
- a nut with soft, milky inside and a hard, hairy shell
- a small, round, red fruit
- having stature and influence like a chief
- a comfortable seat with back and arms for 2–3 people
- a small brown animal with spikes on its back
- healthy, rosy-faced, confident
- lizard that can change the colour of its skin to match its surroundings
- has a sharp taste, a small axe
- a stone carving of ugly person with water coming out of its mouths
- a child
- a person successful in business who has become rich and famous
- someone speaking without moving their lips, as if the voice comes from a dummy

COLUMN1: WORD	COLUMN 2: WHAT IT MEANS
1 cockroach	
2 tomahawk	
3 gargoyle	
4 mana	
5 hedgehog	
6 chameleon	
7 sanguine	
8 mokopuna	
9 vinegar	
10 ventriloquist	
11 tomato	
12 sofa	
13 coconut	
14 sputnik	
15 tycoon	

Activity 8.8: Thesaurus activity—synonyms and antonyms

The words below are from a *School Journal* story called "Fernando Saves the Day", reading level 9.5–10.5 years. Use the thesaurus to find synonyms and antonyms.

KEY WORD	SYNONYMS	ANTONYMS
excited		
greedy		
delicious		
beautiful		
yucky		
miserably		
properly		
accidentally		
concentrate		

CHAPTER 9

Reflections

In the teaching of English, a major objective of *The New Zealand Curriculum* (Ministry of Education, 2007), and the *Reading and Writing Standards* (Ministry of Education, 2009), is for students to be able to use "an increasing vocabulary to make meaning". The aim of this book has been to present five strategies that every reader can use to achieve this objective. They are the "high 5": print exposure and using context clues while reading; breaking words into meaningful parts; organising and structuring information about new words; exploring the multiple meanings of polysemous words and figurative language; and using the dictionary and thesaurus.

We began the book with a short history of English. This knowledge, explained in Chapter 1, is invaluable when teaching and learning about words. Knowing where words such as *cat*, *rabbit*, *inspector*, *inhospitable*, *biology* and *photograph* come from as well as the characteristics of their origins (i.e., Anglo-Saxon, Latin and Greek) helps the reader understand words better. Children should begin learning about the history of English during their junior school years. "The Wandering Heartbeat" (McCallum, 2001), a story written at the seven-year-old level includes both Latin (*ambulance*—from Latin *amulate*, to move about; *hospital*—from Latin *hospes*, guest; *monitor*—from Latin *monere*, to warn) and Greek (*television* and *telemeter*) words. While Latin- and Greek-based words are not common in junior-level texts, teaching children at an early age prepares them for when they do encounter Latin and Greek words in upper primary and secondary school.

Where would we be without words? Words are "the core ingredient in language". Chapter 2 focused on what it means to know a word and how words are learnt.

Chapter 3 discussed how teachers can cater for children who do not have English as their first language. This is a really important topic. New Zealand's colonial history has from the beginning had children and adults learning English as an additional language. At least two languages, English and Māori, were spoken in this country from the very beginning of the British invasion of New Zealand. In the 21st century nearly all Māori children are bilingual or speak English as their first language but waves of recent immigration have meant that there are nowadays many children in classrooms whose first language is not English.

Some newer teachers might find it difficult to remember a time when New Zealand classrooms did not have new immigrant children learning English as an additional language. In actual fact it was not that long ago. We recall a large intermediate school in the Waikato in the late 1980s when a brother and sister arrived—neither spoke English. The principal faced the challenge of placing the two children with a teacher who had the skills to teach English to non-English speakers. Not one teacher had taught English to non-English speaking students. Twenty years later it is the norm to have children learning English as an additional language in New Zealand classrooms. In some schools more than 30 languages are spoken. Many of these clever children speak English at school and Spanish, Chinese, Korean, Afrikans, Samoan etc. before and after school.

Chapters 4, 5, 6, 7 and 8 focus on teaching vocabulary. These chapters are full of practical ideas on how to explicitly teach vocabulary strategies. We have taught both pre and inservice teachers how to teach the vocabulary strategies discussed in Chapters 4–8. We have also taught students the vocabulary strategies. Native and non-native English-speaking students worked together to unpack English: the Anglo-Saxon words with their compound words and simple prefixes and suffixes, the Latin layer with its prefixes, roots (base words) and suffixes, the Greek layer, as well as strategies for explaining meanings such as concept maps, strategies that show the linkages between different words, such as synonyms and antonyms, homonyms and the figurative side of vocabulary, such as similes, metaphors and much more. Students we taught found the daily "word work" activities to be a fun-filled 20 minutes. We believe students can become "word wizards" if the door is opened for them. For many, words are simply a sea of letters. Meaning is not necessarily attached to the letters. It need not be this way. Explicit teaching of vocabulary strategies and print exposure are necessary if students' vocabularies are to grow at the rate needed to become proficient receivers and producers of language.

Hart and Risley's (2003) landmark study indicated that children who enter school having heard 30,000,000 more words than their classmates, have larger vocabularies than those who haven't. In turn the 30 million Word Club children are more likely to get off to a better start in reading than children who do not belong to the club. Cunningham and Stanovich (1998) found that vocabulary in Grade 2 (about eight years) is a reliable predictor of academic performance in Grade 11 (17 years). We argue that printed text is the richest source of vocabulary beyond the age of 10. We also argue that students need to be explicitly taught vocabulary strategies. Readers may not infer the structure of English through print exposure. Students may not infer that many common words have multiple meanings. Students will be confused if they assign *one* meaning to the word *bank* and then use the one meaning to gain meaning from the following sentences: *I went to the bank to deposit the*

REFLECTIONS

cheque. I sat on the bank and ate lunch. The pilot banked the plane. Vocabulary strategies need to be explicitly taught.

Finally, Michael Pressley and his colleagues have conducted many studies on the nature of effective instruction (see Pressley, Disney, & Anderson, 2007 for a review). Their studies have found that effective teachers do teach vocabulary. Pressley et al. (2007, p. 223) also concluded, based on a number of studies, that there is "room for improvement with respect to vocabulary instruction even in effective classrooms". We believe that the vocabulary strategies outlined in this book are effective.

References

Anderson, R. C., & Freebody, P. (1981). Vocabulary knowledge. In J. T. Guthrie (Ed.), *Comprehension and teaching: Research reviews* (pp. 77-117). Newark, DE: International Reading Association.

August, D., & Shanahan, T. (Eds.). (2006). *Executive summary: Developing literacy in second-language learners: Report of the National Literacy Panel on language-minority children and youth.* Mahwah, NJ. Lawrence Erlbaum.

Balmuth, M. (2009). *The roots of phonics*. (Rev. ed.) Baltimore, MA: Paul H Brookes.

Barnett, L. (1962). The English language. *LIFE, 52*(9), 73-77.

Baugh, A. C., & Cable, T. (2002). *A history of the English language* (5th ed.). London: Routledge.

Baumann, J. F., & Kame'enui, E. J. (2004). *Vocabulary instruction: Research to practice*. New York: Guilford Press.

Beal, G. (2000). *Word origins*. London: Kingfisher.

Beck, I., & McKeown, M. G. (1991). Conditions of vocabulary acquisition. In R. Barr, M. L. Kamil, P. B. Mosenthal, & P. D. Pearson (Eds.), *Handbook of reading research* (Vol. 2, pp. 789-814). White Plains, NY: Longman.

Beck, I., & McKeown, M. (2007). Different ways for different goals, but keep your eye on the higher verbal goals. In R. K. Wagner, A. E. Muse, & K. R. Tannenbaum (Eds.), *Vocabulary acquisition: Implications for reading comprehension* (pp. 182-204). New York: Guilford Press.

Beck, I., McKeown, M., & Kucan, L. (2002). *Bringing words to life: Robust vocabulary instruction*. New York: Guilford Press.

Beck, I. M., McKeown, M. G., & Omanson, R. C. (1987). The effects and use of diverse vocabulary instruction techniques. In M. G. McKeown & M. E. Curtis (Eds.), *The nature of vocabulary acquisition* (pp. 147-163). Hillsdale, NJ: Lawrence Erlbaum.

Beers, G. K. (1996). No time, no interest, no way: The 3 voices of aliteracy (Part 2), *School Library Journal*, 110-113.

Biemiller, A. (2005). Size and sequence in vocabulary development. In E. H. Hiebert & M. L. Kamil (Eds.), *Teaching and learning vocabulary: Bringing research to practice* (pp. 223-242). Mahwah, NJ: Lawrence Erlbaum.

Biemiller, A., & Slonim, N. (2001). Estimating root word vocabulary growth in normative and advantaged populations: Evidence for a common sequence of vocabulary acquisition. *Journal of Educational Psychology, 93*, 498-520.

Blachowicz, C. L. Z., & Fisher, P. (2000). Vocabulary instruction. In M. L. Kamil, P. B. Mosenthal, P. D. Pearson, & R. Barr (Eds.), *Handbook of reading research* (Vol. 3, pp. 503-523). Mahwah, NJ: Lawrence Erlbaum.

Blachowicz, C., & Fisher, P. (2002). *Teaching vocabulary in all classrooms* (2nd ed.). Columbus, OH: Merrill Prentice Hall.

Bloomfield, M. W., & Newmark, L. (1963). *A linguistic introduction to the history of English*. New York: Alfred A. Knopf.

Bryant, P., & Nunes, T. (2004). Morphology and spelling. In T. Nunes & P. Bryant (Eds.), *Handbook of children's literacy* (pp. 91-118). London: Kluwer.

Bryson, B. (1991). *Mother tongue: The English language*. London: Penguin.

Buckland, S. (1992). *Rudy*. Auckland: Magari.

Calfee, R. C., & Associates (1984). *The book: Components of reading instruction*. Unpublished manuscript, School of Education, Stanford University, California.

REFERENCES

Calfee, R. C., & Drum, P. A. (1986). Research on teaching reading. In M. Wittrock (Ed.), *Handbook of research on teaching* (pp. 804–849). New York: Macmillan.

Calfee, R. C., & Patrick, C. L. (1995). *Teach our children well: Bringing K-12 education into the 21st century*. Stanford, CA: Stanford Alumni.

Carey, S., & Bartlett, E. (1978). Acquiring a single new word. *Proceedings of the Stanford Child Language conference, 15*, 17–29.

Carroll, J. B., Davies, P., & Richman, B. (1971). *The American heritage word frequency book.* Boston, MA: Houghton Mifflin.

Chall, J. S., Jacobs, V. A., & Baldwin, L. E. (1990). *The reading crisis: Why poor children fall behind.* Cambridge, MA: Harvard University Press.

Claiborne, R. (1983). *Our marvellous native tongue.* New York: Times Books.

Cleary, B. P. (2005). *How much can a bare bear bear?* Minneapolis, MN: Millbrook Press.

Cleary, B. P. (2006). *Stop and go, yes and no. What is an antonym?* Minneapolis, MN: Millbrook Press.

Coelho, E. (2004). *Adding English: A guide to teaching in multilingual classrooms.* Toronto: Pippin.

Crooks, T., Smith, T., & Flockton, L. (2009). *National Education Monitoring Project: Reading and speaking: Assessment results 2008.* Dunedin: Educational Assessment Research Unit, University of Otago.

Crowther, R. (2005). *Opposites.* London: Walker Books.

Cunningham, A. E., & Stanovich, K. E. (1998). What reading does for the mind. *American Educator, 22*(1 & 2), 8–15.

Cunningham, A. E., & Stanovich, K. E. (1990). Assessing print exposure and orthographic processing skill in children: A quick measure of reading experience. *Journal of Educational Psychology, 82*, 733–740.

Dahl, M. (2007). *If you were a synonym.* Minneapolis, MN: Picture Window Books.

Dale, E., & O'Rourke, J. (1981). *Living word vocabulary.* Chicago: World Book/Childcraft International.

Dale, E., & O'Rourke, J. (1986). *Vocabulary building.* Columbus, OH: Zaner-Bloser.

Darr, C., McDowall, S. Ferral, H., Twist, J., & Watson, V. (2008). *Progressive Achievement Test: Reading.* Wellington: New Zealand Council for Educational Research.

Deverson T. (Ed). (1998). *The New Zealand Oxford paperback dictionary.* Oxford: Oxford University Press.

Donaldson, M. (2010, March 21). *Spelling bee puts the hard word on the Star*Times*, p. A2.

Duder, T. (1995). Swimming: Then and now. In *Choices*, Sport (pp. 2–7). Wellington: Learning Media.

Dunn, L. M., & Dunn, D. M. (2007). *Peabody Picture Vocabulary Test: IV.* Minneapolis, MN: Pearson Assessments.

Durkin, D. (1983). *Teaching them to read.* Boston, MA: Allyn & Bacon.

Dymock, S. J. (2008, July). *An observational and interview study of teachers who are nominated by their principals as exemplary teachers of reading.* [PowerPoint] Paper presented at the meeting of New Zealand Reading Association, Hamilton, New Zealand.

Dymock, S. J., & Nicholson, T. (2007). *Teaching text structures: A key to nonfiction reading success.* New York: Scholastic.

Ehri, L. C. (2005a). Development of sight word reading: Phases and findings. In M. Snowling & C. Hulme (Eds.), *The science of reading: A handbook* (pp. 135–154). Oxford: Blackwell.

Ehri, L. C. (2005b). Learning to read words: Theory, findings and issues. *Scientific Studies of Reading, 9*, 167–188.

Ehri, L. C., & Rosenthal, J. (2007). Spellings of words: A neglected facilitator of vocabulary learning. *Journal of Literacy Research, 39*, 389–409.

Elley, W. B. (1989). Vocabulary acquisition from listening to stories. *Reading Research Quarterly, 24*, 174–187.

Elley, W. B. (2000). *STAR: Supplementary Test of Achievement in Reading: Years 4–6*. Wellington: New Zealand Council for Educational Research.

Elley, W. B. (2001). *STAR: Supplementary Test of Achievement in Reading: Years 7–9*. Wellington: New Zealand Council for Educational Research.

Fitzgerald, J. (1995). English-as-a-second-language reading instruction in the United States: A research review. *Journal of Reading Behavior, 27*, 115–152.

Fox, M. (2001) *Reading Magic*. Sydney: Pan Macmillan.

Fractor, J. S., Woodruff, M. C., Martinez, M., & Teale, W. H. (1993). Let's not miss opportunities to promote voluntary reading: Classroom libraries in the elementary school. *The Reading Teacher, 46*, 476–484.

Freeborn, D. (1998). *From old English to standard English* (2nd ed.). London: Macmillan.

Fukkink, R. G., & de Glopper, K. (1998). Effects of instruction in deriving word meaning from context: A meta-analysis. *Review of Educational Research, 68*, 450–469.

Funk, C. E., & Funk, C. E. Jr. (1958). *Horse-feathers and other curious words*. New York: Harper.

Garcia, G. E. (1991). Factors influencing the English reading test performance of Spanish-speaking Hispanic children. *Reading Research Quarterly, 26*, 371–392.

Garcia, G. E. (2003). The reading comprehension development and instruction of English-language learners. In A. P. Sweet & C. E. Snow (Eds.), *Rethinking reading comprehension* (pp. 30–50). New York: Guilford Press.

Gleitzman, M. (2002). *Boy overboard*. London: Penguin.

Goerss, B., Beck, I., & McKeown, M. (1999). Increasing remedial students' ability to derive word meaning from context. *Reading Psychology, 20*, 151–175.

Gough, P. B., & Tunmer, W. E. (1986). Decoding, reading, and reading disability. *Remedial and Special Education, 7*, 6–10.

Graves, M. F. (2006). *The vocabulary book: Learning and instruction*. New York: Teachers College Press.

Graves, M. F., Slater, W. H., & White, T. G. (1989). Teaching content area vocabulary. In D. Lapp., J. Flood, & N. Farnan (Eds.), *Content area reading and learning* (pp. 214–224). Englewood Cliffs, NJ: Prentice-Hall.

Gwynne, F. (1970). *The king who rained*. New York: Windmill Books.

Gwynne, F. (1976). *A chocolate moose for dinner*. New York: Windmill Books.

Gwynne, F. (1988). *A little pigeon toad*. New York: Simon & Schuster.

Hart, B., & Risley, T. R. (1995). *Meaningful differences in the everyday experience of young American children*. Baltimore, MD: Paul H. Brookes.

Hart, B., & Risley, T. R. (2003). The early catastrophe. *American Educator, 27*(1), 4–9.

Hattie, J. A. (2009). *Visible learning: A synthesis of over 800 meta-analyses relating to achievement*. New York: Routledge.

Hawkins, M. (2005). ESL in elementary education. In E. Hinkel (Ed.), *Handbook of research in second language teaching and learning* (pp. 25–44). Mahwah, NJ: Lawrence Erlbaum.

Hayes, D. P., & Ahrens, M. G. (1988). Vocabulary simplification for children: A case of "motherese"? *Journal of Child Language, 15*, 395–410.

Helman, L. (2009). English words needed: Creating research-based vocabulary instruction for English learners. In M. F. Graves (Ed.), *Essential readings on vocabulary instruction* (pp. 124–140). Newark, DE: International Reading Association.

REFERENCES

Henry, M. K. (2003). *Unlocking literacy: Effective decoding and spelling instruction.* Baltimore, MA: Paul H. Brookes.

Henry, M. K. (1990). *WORDS: Integrated decoding and spelling instruction based on word origin and word structure.* Austin, TX: PRO-ED.

Hirsch, E. D. (2003, Spring). Reading comprehension requires knowledge of words and the world. *American Educator, 27*(1), 10–13, 16–22, 28–29, 48.

Jackendoff, R. (2002). *Foundations of language: Brain, meaning, grammar, evolution.* Oxford: Oxford University Press.

Johnson, D. D., & Johnson, B. (1993). Vocabulary development. In C. J. Gordon, G. D. Labercane, & W. R. McEachern (Eds.), *Elementary reading: Process and practice* (pp. 212–226). Needham Heights, MA: Ginn Press.

Johnson, D. D., Moe, A. J., & Baumann, J. F. (1983). *The Ginn word book for teachers: A basic lexicon.* Lexington, MA: Ginn.

Johnson, D. D., & Pearson, P. D. (1984). *Teaching reading vocabulary* (2nd ed.). New York: Holt, Rinehart, & Winston.

Juel, C. (1988). Learning to read and write: A longitudinal study of 54 children from first through fourth grades. *Journal of Educational Psychology, 80,* 437–447.

King, D. H. (2000). *English isn't crazy!* Timonium, MD: York Press.

Labov, W. (1973). The boundaries of words and their meanings. In C. J. Bailey & R. Shuy (Eds.), *New ways of analyzing variation in English* (pp. 340–373). Washington: Georgetown University Press.

Levin, J. R. (1996). Stalking the wild mnemos: Research that's easy to remember. In G. G. Brannigan (Ed.), *The enlightened educator: Research adventures in our schools* (pp. 85–110). New York: McGraw Hill.

Loewen, N. (2007). *If you were an antonym.* Minneapolis, MN: Picture Window Books.

MacNeil, R., & Cran, W. (2005). *Do you speak American?* Orlando, FL: Harcourt.

McCallum, V. (2001). The wandering heartbeat. *Junior Journal, 23,* 22–25.

McCrum, R. (1987). *The story of English.* London: Faber.

McCrum, R., Cran, W., & MacNeil, R. (1987). *The story of English.* London: Faber and Faber.

McKeown, M., Beck, I., Omanson, R. C., & Pople, M. T. (1985). Some effects of the nature and frequency of vocabulary instruction on the knowledge and use of words. *Reading Research Quarterly, 20,* 522–535.

Ministry of Education. (2007). *The New Zealand curriculum for English-medium teaching and learning in years 1–13.* Wellington: Learning Media.

Ministry of Education. (2009). *National standards for reading and writing.* Wellington: Learning Media.

Ministry of Education. (2010). *Literacy learning progressions: Meeting the reading and writing demands of the curriculum.* Wellington: Learning Media.

Moseley, D. (2001). *ACE spelling dictionary. Find words quickly and improve your spelling.* Grand Rapids, MI: LDA.

Moats, L. C. (2000). *Speech to print: Language essentials for teachers.* Baltimore, MD: Paul H. Brookes.

Mullis, I. V. S., Martin, M. O., Kennedy, A. M., & Foy, P. (2007). *PIRLS 2006 International report: IEA's progress in international reading literacy study in primary schools in 40 countries.* Chestnut Hill, MA: TIMSS & PIRLS International Study Center, Lynch School of Education, Boston College.

Nagy, W. E. (1988). *Teaching vocabulary to improve reading comprehension.* Newark, DE: International Reading Association.

Nagy, W. E. (1997). On the role of context in first- and second-language vocabulary learning. In N. Schmitt & M. McCarthy (Eds.), *Vocabulary: Description, acquisition and pedagogy* (pp. 64–83). Cambridge, UK: Cambridge University Press.

Nagy, W. E. (2007). Metalinguistic awareness and the vocabulary–comprehension connection. In R. R. Wagner, A. E. Muse, & K. R. Tannenbaum (Eds.), *Vocabulary acquisition: Implications for reading comprehension* (pp. 52–77). New York: Guilford Press.

Nagy, W. E., & Anderson, R. C. (1984). How many words are there in printed school English? *Reading Research Quarterly, 19*, 304–330.

Nagy, W. E., Anderson, R. C., & Herman, P. A. (1987). Learning word meanings from context during normal reading. *American Educational Research Journal, 24*, 237–270.

Nagy, W. E., & Herman, P. A. (1987). Breadth and depth of vocabulary knowledge: Implications for acquisition and instruction. In M. McKeown & M. Curtis (Eds.), *The nature of vocabulary acquisition* (pp. 19–35). Hillsdale, NJ: Erlbaum.

Nagy, W. E., & Scott, J. A. (2000). Vocabulary processes. In M. L. Kamil, P. B. Mosenthal, P. D. Pearson, & R. Barr (Eds.), *Handbook of reading research* (Vol. 3, pp. 269–294). Mahwah, NJ: Lawrence Erlbaum.

Nathanson, S., Pruslow, J., & Levitt, R. (2008). The reading habits and literacy attitudes of inservice and prospective teachers. *Journal of Teacher Education, 59*, 313–321. doi10.1177/0022487108321685.

Nation, I. S. P. (1990). *Teaching and learning vocabulary*. Boston, MA: Heinle & Heinle.

Nation, I. S. P. (2001). *Learning vocabulary in another language*. Cambridge, UK: Cambridge University Press.

Nation, I. S. P. (2005). Teaching and learning vocabulary. In E. Hinkel (Ed.), *Handbook of research in second language teaching and learning* (pp. 581–595). Mahwah, NJ. Lawrence Erlbaum.

National Reading Panel. (2000). *Teaching children to read: An evidence-based assessment of the scientific research literature on reading and its implications for reading instruction: Reports of the subgroups* [NIH Publication No. 00-4754]. Washington, DC: National Institute of Child Health and Human Development.

National Reading Research Center. (1994). In their own words: What elementary students have to say about motivation to read. *The Reading Teacher, 48*, 176–178.

Nicholson, T. (1985). The confusing world of high school reading. *Journal of Reading, 28*, 514–526.

Nicholson, T., & Whyte, B. (1992). Matthew effects in learning new words while listening to stories. In C. K. Kinzer & D. J. Leu (Eds.), *Literacy research, theory and practice: Views from many perspectives* (pp. 499–503). Chicago: National Reading Conference.

Nilsen, A., & Nilsen, D. F. (2006). Latin revived: Source-based vocabulary lessons courtesy of Harry Potter. *Journal of Adolescent and Adult Literacy, 50*, 128–134.

Nist, J. (1966). *A structural history of English*. New York: St. Martin's Press.

Nunes, T., & Bryant, P. (2006). *Improving literacy by teaching morphemes*. London: Routledge.

Nunes, T., & Bryant, P. (2009). *Children's reading and spelling: Beyond the first steps*. Chichester, England: Wiley-Blackwell.

Parish, P. (1963). *Amelia Bedelia*. New York: Harper & Row.

Perfetti, C. A., Marron, M. A., & Foltz, P. W. (1996). Sources of comprehension failure: Theoretical perspectives and case studies. In C. Cornoldi & J. Oakhill (Eds.), *Reading comprehension difficulties: Process and intervention* (pp. 137–165). Mahwah, NJ: Lawrence Erlbaum.

REFERENCES

Petrosky, A. R. (1980). The inferences we make: Children and literature. *Language Arts, 57,* 149–156.

Piaget, J. (1955). *The language and thought of the child.* New York: Meridian.

Potter, S. (1966). *Our language.* Middlesex, England: Penguin.

Pressley, M. (2000). What should comprehension instruction be the instruction of? In M. L. Kamil., P. B. Mosenthal, P. D. Pearson, & R. Barr (Eds.), *Handbook of reading research* (Vol. 3, pp. 545–561). Mahwah, NJ: Lawrence Erlbaum.

Pressley, M. (2006). *Reading instruction that works: The case for balanced teaching* (3rd ed.). New York: Guilford Press.

Pressley, M., Disney, L., & Anderson, K. (2007). Landmark vocabulary instructional research and the vocabulary research that makes sense now. In R. K. Wagner, A. E. Muse, & K. R. Tannenbaum (Eds.), *Vocabulary instruction: Implications for reading comprehension* (pp. 205–232). New York: Guilford Press.

Presson, L. (2005). *What in the world is a homophone?* New York: Barron's.

Rosenthal, J. (2009). *Orthography has mnemonic value for learning vocabulary words. Seeing spellings during word study helps elementary students learn new vocabulary words.* Saarbrucken, Germany: VDM Verlag Dr. Muller.

Rosenthal, J., & Ehri, L. C. (2008). The mnemonic value of orthography for vocabulary learning. *Journal of Educational Psychology, 100,* 175–191.

Rowling, J. K. (1997). *Harry Potter and the philosopher's stone.* London: Bloomsbury Publishing.

Rushdie, S. (2001). *Fury.* London: Random House.

Sachar, L. (1998). *Holes.* London: HarperCollins.

Samuels, S. J. (1987). Factors that influence listening and reading comprehension. In R. Horowitz & S. J. Samuels (Eds.), *Comprehending oral and written language* (pp. 295–325). London: Academic Press.

Schmitt, N., & Marsden, R. (2006). *Why is English like that?* Ann Arbor, MI: University of Michigan Press.

Senechal, M., Ouellette, G., & Rodney, D. (2006). The misunderstood giant: On the predictive role of early vocabulary to future reading. In D. K. Dickinson & S. B. Neuman (Eds.), *Handbook of early literacy resea*rch (Vol. 2, pp. 173–182). New York: Guilford Press.

Shannon, G. (1993). Plants that store water. *School Journal, 2*(3), 10–13.

Shea, A. (2008). *Reading the OED: One man, one year, 21,730 pages.* Camberwell, Victoria: Viking.

Snow, C. W., Burns, M. S., & Griffin, P. (Eds.). (1998). *Preventing reading difficulties in children.* Washington, DC: National Academy Press.

Stahl, S. A. (1983). Differential word knowledge and reading comprehension. *Journal of Reading Behavior, 15,* 33–50.

Stahl, S. A. (1985). To teach a word well: A framework for vocabulary instruction. *Reading World, 24,* 16–27.

Stahl, S. A. (1986). Three principles of effective vocabulary instruction. *Journal of Reading, 19,* 662–668.

Stahl, S. A. (2005). Four problems with teaching word meanings. In E. H. Hiebert & M. L. Kamil (Eds.), *Teaching and learning vocabulary* (pp. 95–114). Mahwah, NJ: Lawrence Erlbaum.

Stahl, S. A., & Fairbanks, M. M. (1986). The effects of vocabulary instruction: A model-based meta-analysis. *Review of Educational Research, 56,* 72–110.

Stahl, S. A., & Nagy, W. E. (2006). *Teaching word meanings*. Mahwah, NJ: Lawrence Erlbaum.

Stahl, S. A., & Stahl, K. D. (2004). Word wizards all!: Teaching word meanings in preschool and primary education. In J. F. Baumann & E. J. Kame'enui (Eds.), *Vocabulary instruction: Research to practice* (pp. 59–78). New York: Guilford Press.

Stanovich, K. E. (1986). Matthew effects in reading: Some consequences of individual differences in the acquisition of literacy. *Reading Research Quarterly, 21*, 360-406.

Stanovich, K. E. (1993). Does reading make you smarter? Literacy and the development of verbal intelligence. In H. Reese (Ed.), *Advances in child development and behavior* (Vol. 25, pp. 133-180). San Diego: Academic Press.

Stanovich, K. E. (2000). *Progress in understanding reading*. New York: Guilford Press.

Steig, W. (1971). *Amos and Boris*. Middlesex, England: Penguin.

Sternberg, R. J. (1987). Most vocabulary is learned from context. In M. G. McKeown & M. E. Curtis (Eds.), *The nature of vocabulary acquisition* (pp. 89-105). Hillsdale, NJ: Erlbaum.

Teale, W. H. (2003). Reading aloud to young children as a classroom instructional activity: Insights from research. In A. V. Kleeck, S. A. Stahl, & E. B. Bauer (Eds.), *On reading books to children* (pp. 114-139). Mahwah, NJ: Lawrence Erlbaum.

Terban, M. (2007). *Eight ate: A feast of homonym riddles*. New York: Clarion Books.

Thorndike, E. L. (1917). Reading as reasoning. *Journal of Educational Psychology, 8*, 512–518.

Tompkins, G. E., & Blanchfield, C. (2008). *Teaching vocabulary: 50 creative strategies, grades 6–12*. Columbus, OH: Pearson.

Trelease, J. (2006). *The read-aloud handbook* (6th ed.). New York: Penguin.

Trigwell, A. (2009). Arach-attack! *Orbit—The School Magazine, 94*, 20-23.

Wagner, R. F., & Wagner, M. H. (1961). *Stories about family names*. Portland, ME: J. Weston Walch.

Ward, R. (1997). Book Sell ... in the classroom language programme. *Reading Forum New Zealand, 2*, 22–23.

West, M. (1953). *A General Service List of English words*. London: Green & Co.

White, E. B. (1952). *Charlotte's web*. London: Puffin.

Winchester, S. (2003). *The meaning of everything: The story of the Oxford English dictionary*. Oxford: Oxford University Press.

Worthy, J., Moorman, M., & Turner, M. (1999). What Johnny likes to read is hard to find in school. *Reading Research Quarterly, 34*, 12–27.

Yopp, J. J., & McAdams, K. C. (2007). *Reaching audiences: A guide to media writing*. Boston, MA: Pearson.

www.ingramcontent.com/pod-product-compliance
Lightning Source LLC
Chambersburg PA
CBHW080848010526
44114CB00018B/2396